TO THE MARINKO

Welcome to our practice! We
are all here to serve you
and your dental needs. Please
enjoy this book with
our complements.

In Service,

Dr. Michael D. Stern & "Team"

08/11/2015

Praise for *Beating All Odds*

"This fast-moving, impactful book shows you how to do things that can dramatically increase your odds and chances of success in every area of your personal and business life."

Brian Tracy
International Best-Selling Author of *Create Your Own Future*

"Trying to beat the odds in today's sluggish climate can be frustrating and slow. This book offers many proven and effective strategies that can help transform and propel your efforts."

Dr. Stephen R. Covey
Author, *The 7 Habits of Highly Effective People* and *The Leader in Me*

"In a time when too few of us believe our personal choices have any effect upon our lives, Dr. Taylor Clark offers real-life, specific steps to 'beating the odds' and to mastering the world around us."

Hyrum W. Smith
Co-Founder, FranklinCovey
Founder, Galileo Initiative

"Dr. Clark is a true inspiration to anyone who has been told, 'No, you can't.'"

T. Harv Eker
Author of the #1 *New York Times* Bestseller *Secrets of the Millionaire Mind*

"If you are serious about reaching your goals, then you must read *Beating All Odds*!"

Bill Bartmann
Billionaire Business Coach, www.billbartmann.com

"WOW! I could not put this book down. If you're ready to take your life to a much higher, positive level, then read and use the strategies in this awesome book by my friend Taylor Clark!"

James Malinchak
Co-Author, *Chicken Soup for the College Soul*
"America's Achievement Coach™"
Founder, www.BigMoneySpeaker.com

"Put simply, *Beating All Odds* is life-changing. Taylor Clark's strategies and insights will empower you to take action and make decisions that will propel you towards achieving your full potential and higher realms of success. If you aspire to achieve more, no matter what challenges you may be facing, you need to read this book."

Ivan Misner
New York Times Bestselling Author and Founder of BNI

"If you want to live your dreams, this book will inspire you and show you how to make your dreams become a reality!"

Leslie Householder
Bestselling Author of *The Jackrabbit Factor*

"If you're ready to move to the next level of success, then read this book!"

Richard Paul Evans
#1 *New York Times* Bestselling Author

"I have read more than 1,500 personal and business development books and *Beating All Odds* is clearly one of the best!"

Patrick Snow
International Bestselling Author of *Creating Your Own Destiny*

"*Beating All Odds* is your road map to personal and business success!"

Susan Friedmann, CSP
Author of *Riches in Niches*

A SUCCESS ROAD MAP FOR HIGH ACHIEVERS

BEATING ALL ODDS

Discover Exactly How You Can Succeed in Business and Life

AVIVA
PUBLISHING
NEW YORK

DR. TAYLOR CLARK

DEDICATION

To my beautiful wife, Jannie: Thank you for supporting me and my many endeavors over the years! I appreciate your sticking with me through both the good times and the bad. I love you dearly!

To my children, Tylor, Taylie, Coleton, T.J., Jaymon and Ray: You are the reason I work so hard. This book was written for you. I hope that long after my time, you and your children will benefit from this life fulfilling message. I love you all!

To my parents, Jay Dee and Coleen Clark: You are the best parents a child could ask for. I have become the person I am today because of you. Thank you for all your words of encouragement throughout my entire life. I was always listening! I have benefited not only from all you have given me, but mostly from all you have taught me. I love you both!

To you, dear reader: It is my honor and privilege to help you discover how to beat any odds that might stand in the way of reaching your dreams!

ACKNOWLEDGMENTS

I want to recognize and thank those who gave me their support, encouragement and belief in my dreams. I also want to thank those listed here who helped me with this book and my career as a speaker, motivator and business entrepreneur:

Nikki Albert, Debbie Allen, James Allen, Kevin Allen, Robert Allen, Alicia Baay, Richard Ballard, Dick Barnes, Bill Bartmann, Carol Boon, Wendy Briggs, Dale Carnegie, Cliff Clark, George Clason, Russell Conwell, Stephen Covey, Bryan Dille, Nikki Dille, James Drake, Steven Edgley, T. Harv Eker, Rich Erickson, Richard Paul Evans, Howard Farran, Anissa Ferguson, Rebecca Fine, Patricia Fripp, Jay Geier, Brian Halle, Mark Victor Hansen, Heath Hendrickson, Debbie Ingersoll, Charisse Inserra, Brett Jacobson, Amy Jones, Robert Kiyosaki, Abbie Lange, James Malinchak, Jeannine Mallory, Og Mandino, John Maxwell, John McLelland, Ivan Misner, Stacy Moon, Earl Nightingale, Woody Oakes, DeDe Puckett, Elizabeth Richards, Rudy Ruettiger, Tana Sampson, Shiloh Schroeder, Michael Schuster, Patrick Snow, Tom Tervort, Bart Thompson, Tyler Tichelaar, Brian Tracy, Todd Vogel, Wallace Wattles, Zig Ziglar.

Contents

FOREWORD
MICHAEL D. STERN, DDS

This book is written for anyone who ever wondered what their worth as a person might be. It is written to help each one of us understand that despite whatever odds seem to stand in our way; our worth as human beings is not diminished - even a little bit.

Dr. Clark describes himself as an average person, yet his personal, family and business related accomplishments are far above average. How does he achieve so much? More importantly, how does he position himself in life to ensure a prosperous future for his family? The answer is simple. He applies true principles to his life and businesses. Beating All Odds plainly teaches these principles.

The principles and strategies taught in Beating All Odds are powerful. Applying what you learn in these pages will dramatically change your life for the better, giving you a huge advantage toward achieving your dreams.

Whether you are one of our friends, students, or patients, it is our sincere hope that this book improves your life and gives you a million reasons to smile.

Warmest Regards,

Michael D. Stern, DDS
Owner, Smile Brighter Willoughby Hills,
home of the Perpetual White Sale™
Owner, Assist To Succeed Dental Assisting School,
Willoughby Hills, Ohio

PREFACE
RUDY RUETTIGER

The odds were stacked against me my whole life. I grew up in a small Midwestern blue collar town. No one in my family had ever gone to college, let alone graduated from college. I had several brothers and sisters, and from a young age, I was never encouraged to dream of big things in life. I was just told, and expected, to do what I could to get through high school and get a job at the local factory.

Growing up, my father passed along one major passion to me that changed my life forever. It was a love and passion for anything to do with the University of Notre Dame, especially Notre Dame football. When I was a child, our family gathered around the television on Saturday afternoons to watch the Fighting Irish play.

I remember the time I stood up and told my family that one day I would play football for the University of Notre Dame. They laughed in my face and told me to look forward to a future working in the factories. As a result of accepting other people's opinions of me growing up, and sizing up my odds, I began to follow other people's plans for my life.

I barely graduated from high school, and sure enough, ended up working in the factory with my best friend. I initially accepted that I was too small, too slow and didn't have the grades to get anywhere near Notre Dame. My conclusions at that point were the same as my family's. For the first four years after high school, I didn't have what it took to beat the odds and play football at Notre Dame.

Then something happened that changed my life. My best friend lost his life in a terrible work accident at the factory. This was the same friend who'd always believed in my dream of playing football for Notre Dame. He'd even bought me a Notre Dame varsity football jacket for my birthday the year before. As a result of that tragedy, I made a decision to beat my odds. Four years later, I was carried off the football field my senior year, something that has never happened again since that day in 1975. Later on in life, I beat the odds again when I risked everything I had to get the award-winning movie *Rudy* made.

Through this process, I have learned we all have an underdog spirit inside us. I learned that no matter what your circumstances are in life, if you believe in your visions, work hard enough and never give up or give in to others' opinions of you, you can beat the odds and achieve all your life's goals. You are in the driver's seat! I learned it takes hard work, determination and a level of belief like never before. I learned that no matter what the odds are, you do have what it takes if you follow your heart and take consistent action on your goals. As a result, you certainly can and will beat all odds.

In this powerful book, *Beating All Odds*, Dr. Taylor Clark shows you how to discover exactly what to do to succeed in life and overcome all odds you might face along the way. Dr. Clark has overcome some tremendous odds in his life—he's been there. He has intensely studied the field of personal growth and development for more than sixteen years. He has simplified the best material available to show you how to find and achieve your goals and dreams, despite any circumstances, challenges or obstacles that might stand in your way.

Dr. Clark helps you determine your ultimate goal in life. He helps you create a plan of action and sets you on the journey to realize your biggest dreams. He breaks it down into bite-size pieces to help you gain the needed confidence, vision and determination to do what few others think you can.

He becomes your partner, accountability coach and guide as you realize your dreams. Dr. Clark has discovered what I learned during the process of becoming a football player at the University of Notre Dame. This secret to success will change your life, allow you to beat the odds and experience the realization of your dreams.

I challenge you to take action on your destiny. Don't just read this book—study it. Carry it with you, memorize the quotes and use it as your daily companion to overcome and conquer any and all odds standing in your way.

I hope you are ready for an exciting journey. This book will change your life and the life of your family for years to come. It will give you the ability to re-write your future and empower you to beat every obstacle standing in your way. If I were a betting man, I'd be willing to place my bet on you beating the odds once you read this book and apply its wisdom to your life.

*Down, set, hike….*The game has begun. You are now playing with the best in the world. Let this book become your playbook and I promise you can beat your biggest competition, which is your own mind and self-limiting beliefs. This book will allow you to score and win in your own game of life.

Looking back at your success ten years from now, you will see it was this book that turned the momentum in your favor. You'll attribute Dr. Clark's book to the first play in the success movie of your life. This life-changing book certainly is the missing piece of the puzzle that will help you beat your odds and soar in life! You may never be the same again.

Rudy Ruettiger

www.RudyInternational.com

Journeying to Higher Ground

"Tough times never last, tough people do!"
— *Robert Schuller*

Over the years of working with and serving thousands of people, I've come to the conclusion that everyone wants a happy and successful life that gets better with time. We want the same for our loved ones. And everyone encounters difficulties along the way that could hold us back. I am a lifelong student of the universal principles of success that work for anyone who uses them. I recently had an experience that beautifully illustrates how using these principles will help anyone beat the odds in life.

It was a very cold, foggy and dreary Saturday in Boise, Idaho. A weather inversion had the entire valley engulfed in a thick fog. It was so cold and ugly that nobody wanted to be outdoors, including me. As the day progressed, my kids became more restless in the house.

Then the phone rang. It was my brother Mike enthusiastically inviting me to grab the three oldest kids and join him and his kids on the slopes at the nearby Bogus Basin Ski Resort for some late afternoon skiing. "You're crazy," I told Mike.

He replied, "No! I just checked the weather up on the slopes and it's sunny, clear blue skies and ten degrees warmer there than it is down here. Let's go!"

I looked out the window and thought, "There's no way." Nevertheless, I accepted his invitation.

We quickly gathered our winter gear and jumped in Mike's SUV. It was ugly. The fog remained thick and the temperature was near freezing. As we arrived at the base of the mountain and began the ascent, it started to look even worse. We pressed forward and gradually made our way up the windy mountain road. I remember watching the car's outdoor temperature display begin to drop. Little snow flurries began to swirl around us as we continued upward.

After driving most of the way up the mountain, the weather looked uglier than when we'd started. I was half tempted to turn around and go back home. But Mike persisted, "Really, that's what the weather report said. They said it was great up there." Still, I even began to sense a little doubt from him!

Something magical happened as we continued our journey to higher ground. When we were about a minute from the resort—poof! We broke through the thick blanket of clouds and saw nothing but sunny blue skies. I gazed at the temperature display again and watched it literally rise ten degrees in a matter of minutes! It was one of the most amazing things I have seen in a long time.

By the time we had ourselves and the kids bundled up and squared away with ski rentals, the sun was beginning to set. We took the chair lift to the top of the mountain and what we saw was absolutely stunning! The entire valley below us was completely covered in a cottony white blanket of thick fog. The blue sky had turned several shades of orange in a spectacular sunset that gently rested on the soft white blanket of fog. The front cover of this book is very similar to what I observed that magical winter day.

Then it hit me. Suddenly, the message of this book became crystal clear. What I had just experienced was a perfect metaphor for life. As we persistently journey to higher ground, we will eventually break free from the bitter cold and clouds that may surround us. Everyone will experience the thick clouds of discouragement and struggle in life. Perhaps at this very moment, you may find yourself engulfed in fog with no sign of sunshine. Maybe life is good but something is holding you back from getting to the next level. Whoever you are, whatever your stage in life, it's time to journey to higher ground. That's the way to overcome those obstacles keeping you from reaching your dreams. As you continuously journey to higher ground, you will be empowered to rise above the clouds of discouragement and beat those odds in life.

Among other things, my life's purpose is to make life better for others. I wrote this book to guide and encourage you courageously to pursue your dreams. I call the thirty chapter headings my "Success Road Map." As you follow this map, I want to be your guide, your friend and your fan. I want to cheer you on as you journey to higher ground and beat all the odds in your life.

Before we begin, I think it's important you know the material for this book was developed through my life experiences, including more than sixteen years of study in personal development, earning a Bachelor of Science degree, becoming a Doctor of Dental Surgery, starting and running several successful businesses, consulting dentists across the U.S., and most importantly, being a husband and father.

I can imagine what some of you may think: "You're a successful doctor. You know lots of influential people. Success comes easy for you. You have no idea what an 'average' person like me has to go through. I'm not smart enough, young enough or talented enough to succeed in the way you suggest. These principles may work for you, but surely they won't work for me."

Whether you believe it or not, you *do have what it takes* to succeed, perhaps as much or more than I do. See, I have considered myself an underdog much of my life. In school, I was always one of the last ones to finish an exam. I wondered why I had to study twice as long as my peers only to achieve the same result—or worse. Unexpected trials, challenges and heartaches have beaten me down. I know what it's like to struggle to get up one more time after being knocked down. In this book, I share many experiences to encourage, inspire and lift you up.

I can also imagine what thoughts might be crossing your mind with the current state of affairs in the world: The economy is so bad, unemployment is so high, the housing situation is the worst it's been in years, the stock market has plummeted, people have too much debt, they're either worried about lay-offs or they don't even have a job. Do you watch the news? Do you read the gloom and doom news articles? Turn the TV off. Turn your mind on to continuous learning and personal development. Choose not to participate in any recession. Instead, see the many opportunities that abound even when the masses proclaim, "The sky is falling."

No matter how thick the dark clouds of despair surrounding you, there is a sure way out: Journey to higher ground. Are you ready to begin? Great! Then let's get started!

SECTION ONE

PREPARE

CHAPTER 1

Know Where You Are Going

"The first principle of success is desire—
knowing what you want."
— Robert Collier

People who are successful in all areas of life have one major thing in common: They know where they are going! They're focused on a destination and they move toward that destination every day of their lives.

We can learn an important lesson from the Disney classic, *Alice in Wonderland*. As Alice wandered along, she encountered the Cheshire Cat. She asked the cat to help her find her way.

"Where do you want to go?" asked the cat.

"I don't know," said Alice.

"Then," said the cat, "it really doesn't matter, does it?"

Which way are you going? Why is it important to know where you are going? Earl Nightingale's answer to this question is the key. The following excerpt comes from *The Strangest Secret* by Earl Nightingale:

Think of a ship leaving a harbor. And think of it with the complete voyage mapped out and planned. The captain and crew know exactly where the ship is going and how long it will take— it has a definite goal. And 9,999 times out of 10,000, it will get there.

Now let's take another ship—just like the first—only let's not put a crew on it, or a captain at the helm. Let's give it no aiming point, no goal, and no destination. We just start the engines and let it go. I think you'll agree that if it gets out of the harbor at all, it will either sink or wind up on some deserted beach—a derelict. It can't go anyplace, because it has no destination and no guidance. It's the same with a human being.

We're all moving toward something in life. We are either moving toward our goals or away from them. If we have no direction and no goals, then there's a good chance we are moving away from where we would ultimately like to be.

WHERE ARE YOU GOING?

Where are you going? Do you know? If so, are you moving closer to or further from your destination? Just taking time to think about what's most important in life brings power. We are empowered when we know what fuels our fire—what we're passionate about. In this very busy thing called life, it's far too easy to miss out on the opportunity to identify exactly where we want to go. Schedule some time now or within the next twenty-four hours just to meditate and think about where you'd like to go. As you do this, think about these words by T.E. Lawrence:

All men dream, but not equally. Those men who dream by night in the dusty recesses of their minds wake in the morning to find it was but vanity, but those men who dream by day—these are dangerous men, for they dream with open eyes to make their dreams come true.

Discovering what you are passionate about will enable you to pinpoint where you want to go. To get started, list your top five reasons for being on this earth. Think about each one and prioritize them from most important to least. This will help you identify your destination or solidify the destination you already knew you had.

What is most important in your life?

_____

_____

_____

_____

_____

_____

_____

What makes these important to you?

_____

_____

_____

_____

_____

_____

_____

AIMING AT THE TARGET

When I was a teenager, I watched the great Denise Parker on TV many times. She was an Olympic archer, and I remember seeing her hit the bull's eye over and over again. I was amazed at how accurate and reliable she was. It seemed she could beat anybody, even the best in the sport.

From the little I know about archery, I know one thing for a fact. I could take you to the park near my house, and in less than twenty minutes, teach you how to beat Denise Parker. And I wouldn't care if you had experience! We could even catch Denise on her very best day and you'd beat her every time. All you'd have to do is follow my instructions. We'd borrow my eleven-year-old son's bow and arrows and let the games begin.

Sound crazy? Before you think I've lost my marbles and wonder why you should even listen to me, let me explain how we'd accomplish this. First, I'd take Denise, blindfold her and spin her around thirty times. Then the contest would begin. You'd aim for the target the best you could, pull back, and release the arrow. After evacuating the neighborhood, we'd have Denise do the same. You'd win every time!

How can you or anyone, even an Olympian, hit a target you cannot see? Even more important, how can you hit a target you don't even have? I guarantee you'll have a far better chance of hitting a target if you have one and if you can see it!

YOUR TARGET: A PERSONAL MISSION STATEMENT

The best way to identify your target in life is to create a personal mission statement. Every successful company or organization has one. Successful individuals and families are likely to have one as well. What is a mission statement? It is a statement that declares what you want to do and what you stand for.

I encourage you to create a personal mission statement. What do you stand for? What do you want to accomplish in life? What drives you to get out of bed each morning? What do you want to be remembered for? What is your major purpose in life?

Ponder these questions and write a paragraph that summarizes your mission, your chief goal in life and the target you focus on every day of your life. Then make a few copies of your mission statement and place it where you'll see it every day. Being able to see your mission statement at least every morning and night will help create TOMA (Top of mind awareness). There is magic in having your target in mind on a constant basis. You'll find your actions and direction will bring you closer to your target much quicker and more often.

MY PERSONAL MISSION STATEMENT

Some years ago, I wrote my personal mission statement and have modified it some since then. It's posted on what I call my "Victory Board," on a prominent wall in our home. It's right where I go to start and end my day. I can't help but see it because it's there before my eyes in bold lettering. It's a constant reminder as to where my focus, energy and actions should go.

MY PERSONAL MISSION STATEMENT

I am a responsible, loving, caring and very successful husband, father and powerfully positive contributor to society. As such, I provide my family with many of the things money can buy and all of the things money can't buy. By succeeding temporally, physically and spiritually, I provide complete freedom for my family, give more to charity and position my family to be of ever greater service to God and our fellow man. Financial freedom allows our family to enjoy life fully, spend time with each other and together serve God and our fellow man without limits.

This mission drives me! It excites me and makes me want to keep plugging away whether things are going well or not. Your mission statement will do the same for you if you create it and post it where you can see it daily.

I have several different businesses. My businesses all happen to have the same mission statement.

MISSION STATEMENT FOR MY BUSINESSES

The purpose of our business is to make life better for people.

SUMMARY

We've discussed the most important elements in beating your odds. Adding a personal mission statement will help increase your chances of success. If you already have a personal mission statement, then now is the time to refocus on it and make sure you reflect upon it often. If you don't have one, then now is the perfect time to create one.

Back when I was about twelve years old, we had a youth activity in church that taught us about being proactive and taking charge of our lives. I don't remember much about the activity, but I remember getting a T-shirt with this anonymous saying on the back:

If not me, who? If not now, when?

My friend, now is the time to take full advantage of the power that comes with a solid mission statement. Use it to guide you along your path and beat the odds.

CHAPTER 2

The Bigger the Why,
The Easier the How

"Build a dream and the dream will build you."
— Robert Schuller

Now that you've identified your big dream, I have a question for you. Do you wonder *how* you will accomplish your life's purpose? Is it so big that the "how" seems out of reach?

Let me share a lesson I learned some years ago from NFL Hall of Famer and Super Bowl champion Mike Singletary. Currently, Mike is head coach of the San Francisco 49ers. Recently, I had an opportunity to see Coach Singletary in person and hear him speak. As he talked about his life, including his childhood, I was surprised to learn about the many obstacles and adversities he faced on his way to success. He shared that he wasn't the fastest or the most gifted athlete in his circle of friends, and he wasn't the best athlete in his family. He was not even picked in the NFL draft until the later rounds.

Though Mike Singletary faced many disadvantages when compared to his competition, he had one thing that very few people have. As I listened to him there on stage, I was captivated by what he said. He talked about his dreams and aspirations and then shared what I feel is one of the reasons for his success. That day, he taught me this lesson:

The bigger the why, the easier the how. It didn't matter that he wasn't the most gifted athlete when compared to his peers. He dominated them at every level because he'd always dreamed of being an NFL player—his red-hot WHY. You're just getting started when you set a big goal and have a big dream. Mike demonstrated he'd clearly identified *why* he wanted to succeed and he was extremely passionate about it. Not only did he become an NFL player, but in 1999, he was included in *The Sporting News* list of the 100 greatest football players.

We all have dreams and aspirations in life, but sometimes the "how" seems to be the tough part. It reminds me of an experience I had when I was about ten years old. Have you ever been challenged to do something you knew would be hard, but at the same time knew it would be good for you? That's what happened to me.

Back then, much to my chagrin today as a dentist, I loved candy. It was one of my favorite things and eating it was sheer pleasure. One day, my dad and brothers issued a challenge they were sure I couldn't complete. They challenged me to go an entire year without candy, with a few exceptions, including Halloween. They were so sure, in fact, each of them backed the challenge with the promise of five dollars at the end. Back then, five dollars was a lot of money to a ten-year-old boy. I knew it would be good for me and I knew I could do it.

I was up for a challenge and told them they were on! The thought of accomplishing something that seemed so difficult and impossible motivated me to meet the challenge. Also, gaining self-confidence and proving the naysayers wrong became more important than any joy I'd get from eating candy. In other words, the "why" was much bigger than the "how." The year flew by and before I knew it, I had three five-dollar bills and a whole lot of self-confidence. To this day, I don't eat very much candy and the confidence gained in that victory helped me achieve much greater things.

Know What You're Fighting For

Cinderella Man is one of my favorite movies. This film tells of the overwhelming life challenges faced by former professional boxer James J. Braddock. He fought professionally before and during the Great Depression. It's an inspiring story because Braddock came to know what he was really fighting for.

Before the Great Depression, Braddock was a good boxer and won many fights. He gained fame, money and the popularity that goes with it. At some point, though, he traded his passion for fame and glory. The lack of drive for success, combined with injuries, led to his demise. Next came the Great Depression. Gone were the legendary days of abundance. Hard economic times beat Braddock and his family to their knees. The once wealthy and successful fighter was destitute. In professional circles, he was viewed as a has-been.

Losing his wealth, having his home utilities turned off, seeing his children go hungry and suffer illness and feeling powerless to do anything about it drove Braddock to the depths of humility and despair. As a result, his passion for boxing was reborn. He identified a red-hot burning "why." Though the odds were stacked against him, he took any job he could find to support his family while he began training. Then a big break came and he landed a fight opportunity. He went into the ring, hungry in more ways than one, and destroyed his opponent.

Against all odds, Braddock fought his way to the top and earned a title bout with Max Baer, the world champion. In the pre-fight press conference, a reporter reminded Braddock of his boxing demise and asked how he had turned things around so dramatically. Braddock's response was poignant. He said that before, he hadn't known what he was fighting for, but that had changed. When the reporter asked what he was fighting for, Braddock responded, "Milk." That one word said it all. He was fighting for his family's very survival. I cannot think of a bigger "why."

As Braddock went on to take the title, he inspired an entire country that had lost all hope. A red-hot burning "why" certainly makes the toughest "how" much more reachable.

GETTING UP WHEN YOU FALL DOWN

The year 2003 was particularly tough for me. I was struggling with a new dental practice that hadn't even been open a year. My wife and I had recently lost her relatively young parents, each to a terminal illness. I'll admit it; I was scared. Each day I looked into the sweet and innocent faces of my wife and three children, I knew I faced mountains of debt and unrelenting bills—seemingly unending challenges. I knew my family depended on me and I had to overcome this mountain of adversity.

I'd picked up a copy of Lance Armstrong's book, *It's Not About The Bike*. He wrote the book after winning his first Tour de France. In 1996, he had cancer and doctors gave him only a forty percent chance of survival. Surviving and beating death became Lance Armstrong's red-hot burning "why." It fueled his victory over cancer and subsequent Tour De France victories. I was heavily inspired as I followed his progress during his fifth Tour De France. I was excited each morning as I grabbed the newspaper to check his progress. It motivated me to be courageous in facing my own adversities.

One day, I read an Associated Press article detailing Armstrong's crash in a late round that threatened to defeat him. Here is an excerpt:

His yellow jersey smeared with dirt after a fall, Lance Armstrong got back on his bike with a fierce look that said it all: The Tour de France is slipping away. It's now or never.

In its 100-year history, the Tour has witnessed many epic days, but few like this. Armstrong went into Monday's 15th stage with his overall lead hanging by a thread. The four-time champion overcame a hard crash and two weeks of lackluster form to cross the line 40 seconds ahead of archrival Jan Ullrich, slumped over his handlebars, drained.

Armstrong, 31, of Texas, widened his overall lead over Ullrich to 67 seconds, setting up cycling's premier race for a gripping finale Sunday in Paris.

Armstrong went on to victory and his fifth consecutive Tour De France. Ultimately, he won a record-setting seven years in a row. His fifth victory, however, was arguably the toughest ever. What's most amazing is knowing he beat all odds by overcoming cancer. Beating death itself gave Lance Armstrong the biggest "why" of all—one that was instrumental in his winning seven consecutive Tour de France Championships.

I clipped that article and picture of determination and have gone back to it many times since. Suddenly, my challenges didn't seem as intimidating as before. After all, if Lance Armstrong could get back on his bike after a hard crash, I could certainly get back on mine.

SUMMARY

Obstacles appear in the path of anyone who wants to succeed. All successful people face—and overcome—obstacles and adversities. How do they do it? A huge "why" drives them to find a way. It will work for you, too. If you focus on "why" you want to accomplish your big dream, you'll attract and recognize the "how" when it appears.

As you continue on your path to achieve your objectives in life, reflect often on why you are doing it. By focusing on the "why," you'll find great strength to carry on and beat any and all odds that get in your way. The road to success is always under construction. The detours, delays and potholes will become smaller and smaller as you focus on your mission and why it is important to you.

CHAPTER 3

Make Family Your Highest Priority

"The happiest moments in my life
have been the few which I have passed
at home in the bosom of my family."
— Thomas Jefferson

Do you regret not spending more time with your family? Do you wish you could just turn back the clock and do things differently? Well, an experience early in my university days taught me a most important lesson.

I knew I wanted to be a doctor of some sort. I just didn't know which health profession was right for me. I took a course where medical doctors from the community spoke about what life was like for them. I'll never forget the doctor who spoke with great regret. The look on his face and his obvious desire for a different past created a somber environment in the room.

Becoming a health professional often requires at least eight (or more) years of university education. The unhappy doctor who spoke to us that day told of the years he missed with his family while he was in medical school and during his residency. He spoke of being gone almost all the time, studying and pouring time into his medical training. On one occasion, he managed to make it home to have dinner with his family. As dinner began, he didn't follow one of the family rules. His young son said to his mother, "Dad doesn't know the family rules." In other words, the little boy was saying this guy named "Dad," the guy who's never home, the guy he didn't really know, was so uninvolved with the family that he didn't even know the family rules. The doctor said he missed precious years of his children's lives, and he'd never get them back. I left that class feeling very discouraged about becoming any type of doctor.

Shortly after that semester, I chose the profession of dentistry. I decided then and there to make family my top priority. I graduated from college and was accepted by Creighton University Dental School. I'd heard about the rigors of dental school, but I was determined to put my family first. First, I decided how much time to put into school. My freshman year set the stage and served as a template for the remaining three years. During the week, I got up early, went to school and studied until 6:00 p.m. Evenings were reserved for my family. On Saturdays, I got up early and studied until 2:00 p.m. The rest of the weekend was devoted to spending time with family.

Today, I have a wonderful wife and six beautiful children. We look back at those dental school years with fondness. Sometimes we even long for those days. They created some of our best family memories. I might not have been at the top of my class, but I was at the top with those who mattered most: my family. Considering the time I'd set aside for the demands of dental school, I did pretty well. During school and study time, my focus and intensity were at a peak. I knew I had to make the hay while the sun was shining.

WHAT ABOUT THAT FAME AND GLORY?

People around the globe found themselves caught up in the excitement of the 2008 Summer Olympics in China. All eyes were focused on the great American swimmer Michael Phelps. The media couldn't get enough of him! Countless news stories, commercials and feature articles highlighted Phelps and his quest to break Mark Spitz's record and win eight gold medals in one Olympics.

Television ratings skyrocketed when swimming events took center stage. I couldn't stay away from the TV, watching Phelps as he racked up successive victories. The excitement and pressure mounted with each gold-medal performance. I remember watching Phelps win his eighth gold medal. The race had been so close; the excitement zoomed around the world! Through the crowds of people celebrating his success, a reporter approached the victorious swimmer. Phelps told the reporter something that has stayed with me. He said he just wanted to see his mom. With each win, and even with the biggest win of all, his heart was with his family.

Everyone wants to succeed in life. Accomplishing our goals and overcoming the odds brings us satisfaction and confidence. But when all is said and done, family is what matters most.

I love Harold B. Lee's unique insight into the significance of families:

> *"The most important work you will ever do will be*
> *done within the walls of your own home."*

Will You Be There?

Do you remember how you felt the last time a member of your family became very sick? Did you wish you could just wave a magic wand and make things all better again? Some years ago, our baby boy was very sick with a fever and all that goes with it. His ever-rising temperature, sweating, difficulty breathing, coughing—all of it—was almost more than I could bear. It was during the early hours of a sleepless night that I felt powerless. How I wished I could go through the illness in place of my dearly loved son.

In that moment, I made a decision. Whenever anyone in my family gets sick or ill, or goes through any major struggle, no matter the gravity, I decided to be there for them. That would mean having control over my time, having adequate money in the bank for future needs, having proper insurance coverage and making it possible to be 100 percent in the moment with that person in the time of need. Being able to provide for his or her physical, financial, and spiritual needs became a top priority more than ever. Since then, I've made every effort to structure my businesses around my family's lives, instead of the other way around.

Today, it's great to know that, come what may, I've done my best to position myself so I can drop what I'm doing and be there for my wife and children should the need arise. They matter most to me. No business deal or outside success is worth not being able to be the champion of my family members' hearts.

CHERISH EACH DAY WITH YOUR LOVED ONES

When I first met my wife Jannie, I saw right away how much fun I'd have with my in-laws. I mean this in a good way! Boating, jet-skiing, camping, and just plain spending time together in the same room was an important part of Jannie's family life. I was happy to fit right in and enjoyed the time we spent together.

Soon I learned that my mother-in law Janet's health was not good. She had severe asthma and was always one small attack away from the hospital. Oxygen tanks, breathing tubes, and nebulizer medical equipment were commonplace for her. Then, shortly after our wedding, Jannie's father, Grant, fell upon hard times with his health. He was diagnosed with a rare bone marrow disorder. After doing research, we found the average life expectancy after diagnosis was only five years.

The thought of possibly losing Jannie's parents in their late forties or early fifties was painful. Together, Jannie and I decided to cherish each day we were given with them. We tried not to focus on our fears of losing them but rather to enjoy each day we were blessed to have them with us. We took lots of trips together and visited them almost every weekend during my final undergraduate years.

Then 2003, the horrible year, arrived. Grant's health took a sudden turn for the worse and deteriorated rather quickly. While we were focused and concerned primarily with him, Janet had an asthma attack in the night and passed away. Seven weeks later, Grant passed away. Oh, how we miss them!

Though it's difficult without them in our lives, we will forever cherish the many memories made when the sun was shining. We have a cherished collection of pictures, scrapbooks, videos and recorded memories of them we reflect upon whenever we choose. Great comfort comes during the difficult moments in mourning their loss because we took advantage of the precious time we had with them.

Life is short. We never know when life will end for ourselves or our loves ones. That's why it's so important to cherish each day we're blessed to have our loved ones with us. Sometimes it's frustrating, but striving to love and cherish our family members every day will bring us tremendous comfort when we no longer have them with us.

I have a great deal of respect for Leigh Brinkerhoff, one of the leaders of my church. He might not even know it, but he taught me a powerful lesson. Leigh is a very successful businessman and was president and COO of the JR Simplot Corporation for several years. Recently, Leigh said he'd been on many important business boards and councils and had been part of some significant international business deals over the years. He paused and gently shook his head as he shared that of all his memories, his family memories stand out most. His memories of big business deals and successes just aren't as clear. He said that in all he's accomplished, family matters most. That was an important lesson for me.

SUMMARY

I love the story of the little boy who eagerly looks out the family room window and waits for his dad to come home from work every day. Finally, he sees the familiar car approach and pull into the driveway. Jumping for joy, he runs to meet his father at the door. Just as the door opens, he screams, "Daddy! I'm so glad you're home! I've been waiting all day! Come on, Dad! Let's go play!"

The father responds, "Son, I'm tired. I need to sit down and rest for a while first. Run along and we'll play later."

"No, Dad! I've waited all day and you're finally home," the little boy replied. "Let's play!"

Again the father said, "Son, Daddy's tired. We'll play later."

The relentless little boy persisted, "Come on, Dad, let's go play!"

Finally, the father glanced over at the end table and saw a magazine. He opened it up and found a picture of the world. He tore it out, ripped it into pieces and gave it to his son, saying, "Okay, you take this picture of the world and tape it back together. When you're finished, we'll play."

To the father's great pleasure, the excited little boy took the magazine pieces and ran off. Proud of himself for his intelligent move, the father sat down to read the paper and relax.

Before long, the boy burst back in the room and exclaimed with excitement, "Okay Dad! Here's the picture of the world, all taped together. Now let's play!"

Perplexed, the father asked, "Son, how on earth did you do that so fast?"

"It was easy," the boy replied. "All I had to do was put the picture of the family together. Once I had the family together, I just flipped it over and the world was all in place, too!"

You see, the family is the fundamental unit of society. The collective strength of our individual families determines the strength and quality of the world we live in. Making your family your top priority will help you and your family—not just at home, but at work and in this ever-challenging society.

CHAPTER 4

Make the Most of Your 86,400

*"Time is what we want most,
but what we use worst."*
— William Penn

Do you make the most of your 86,400? You may know what I'm talking about here or maybe you think I've lost my marbles. You may ask, "What on earth are you talking about, Taylor?"

The staggering truth is the same for every one of us: rich or poor, young or old, male or female, smart or mentally challenged, skinny or fat, etc. We all have a tremendous gift each day in that we are blessed to flip open our eyelids. We have 86,400 seconds every day to make our dreams come true. Think of it! Just realizing we have this gift increases our chances of success. I don't know about you, but 86,400 seconds seems like a pretty significant amount of time to take advantage of all the opportunities out there.

How do you use this time? Do you take advantage of each moment of the day? Do wasted moments pass you by as the clock moves along? I've had more than my fair share of wasted moments, and I'd venture to guess you have, too. Truth is, when we understand how much time we have in the day and realize the many opportunities we have, we can take advantage of those opportunities in many ways.

MAKE THE MOST OF YOUR TIME

How would you spend your time if you knew you only had thirty days to live? Would you do anything differently? How would you treat your loved ones? I love the country music hit "Live Like You Were Dying," by Tim McGraw. Have you heard it? The song is a story about a man in his early forties who is diagnosed with a terminal illness and given a short time left to live. When asked what he did with his remaining time, his response is especially poignant and profound:

> He said I was finally the husband,
> that most the time I wasn't.
> An' I became a friend a friend would like to have
> And all of a sudden goin' fishin,
>
> wasn't such an imposition,
> And I went three times that year I lost my dad
> Well I finally read the Good Book,
>
> and I took a good long hard look
> At what I'd do if I could do it all again…
>
> I went sky diving, I went rocky mountain climbing,
> I went two point seven seconds on a bull named Fu Man Chu.
> And I loved deeper and I spoke sweeter,
> And I gave forgiveness I'd been denying.
> An' he said: Some day, I hope you get the chance,
> To live like you were dyin'.

What must have been going through his mind to cause the man in this song to do what mattered most in his life? Though I'd certainly never wish to have a terminal illness, I do have a saying posted in my home where I can see it every day. It reads: "Make every waking minute count as if you have a terminal illness!" With that mindset, it's very difficult to squander even a few precious moments during the day.

Lance Armstrong really hit me with what he says about this mindset. In his book, *It's Not About the Bike*, mentioned previously, he shares an insight most of us never get. In talking about himself and other cancer victims, he says they are the lucky ones. Lucky to have cancer? Are you kidding me? He goes on to explain how his frame of mind completely changed to give him a most rewarding perspective. When he realized how blessed he was to have a second chance, look at what Lance Armstrong accomplished! Seven Tour De France victories in a row.

DOING TWICE AS MUCH IN HALF THE TIME

On two occasions, I've had the privilege of hearing time management specialist Amy Jones speak about how to do twice as much in half the time. She is a remarkable woman who has accomplished what few have. Her formula for time management is simple, yet powerful. She says that subtracting, adding, multiplying and dividing equals successful management of time. "It all adds up," she says.

First, subtract the "stuff." Get rid of the stuff that steals your time. I like to refer to this stuff as "time vampires." Kill the time vampires! In today's busy world, there is so much competition for our time and attention. If it doesn't help you in your goals and life purpose, then throw it out.

Second, Amy teaches us to add the positives: programs, plans and purpose.

Programs can come in the form of reading instructional books, attending uplifting seminars and implementing success strategies you learn from coaches and mentors.

Plan your work and work your plan. Planning your day the night before allows you to focus on your plan and accomplish so much more.

Purpose brings you back to your personal mission statement. If you know where you're going, you're much more likely to get there.

Third, Amy says to multiply your expectations. Aim high and expect more. We tend to get what we expect, whether we realize it or not. So we might as well aim high. It's okay to go for the big accomplishment rather than settle for mediocrity all the time.

Finally, my favorite part of Amy's formula is to divide. Divide the word "time," and remember to include time for "I" and "me." Taking time to recharge and rejuvenate gets us ready to hit it hard again and effectively go after our goals. This exercise is empowering because it allows us to celebrate our successes and gain a sense of accomplishment.

BECOME REALISTIC ABOUT TV

Zig Ziglar speaks of a study done in a typical manufacturing plant. Looking at the time different levels of workers spent watching television is strikingly insightful. The person who worked by the hour on the line watched an average of thirty hours of TV per week. The person in charge of the line watched an average of twenty-five hours per week. The foreman watched twenty hours per week. The plant superintendent watched twelve to fifteen hours per week. The president watched TV for eight to twelve hours per week. The Chairman of the Board watched four to eight hours and of that, half was spent watching training videos!

Now think about this data Ziglar shared as compared to the findings above.

Forty-seven percent of people feel they don't have enough time to do anything. Yet these same people spend endless hours watching TV. Two days later, they couldn't tell you what they learned. Ziglar suggests if line workers took ten to thirty hours of that TV watching time and got involved with personal growth and development materials, seminars, reading, learning and study, they might not be stuck in permanent jobs on the line. We are not the victims we tend to think we are. There are many things all of us can do to take responsibility and action for our futures.

Now, I'm not purposefully trying to bash TV. However, we really need to think about television and the role it plays in our lives. The biggest harm I see from TV is the time we spend watching it keeps us from doing so many other things to move along the path to achieve our dreams.

Beyond that, watching the news can be one of the most destructive things we can do...especially right before going to bed. I try never to watch the news as the last thing I do before going to bed. What we put into our minds the last twenty minutes before retiring for the night stays in our subconscious mind all night long. The news that sells is usually negative and destructive instead of positive and constructive. Robberies, murders, crimes, the bad economy, the doomsday talk, the hopeless reality of this or that, all paints a picture in our minds that is NOT reality. It's been said that the media accurately predicted twenty-eight of the last two recessions! When we watch mindless television, we give up control of what we allow to enter our minds.

SUMMARY

We all have the same amount of time every day of our lives. How we use that time determines how successful we will be. Beating the odds becomes much easier when you see time as a respected asset.

Benjamin Franklin said, "Dost thou love life? Then waste not time; for time is the stuff life is made of."

When I was a young boy, one of the co-founders of the Franklin Time Management Company introduced me to the concept of time management. He invited me to one of their time management seminars and I learned how to use a day planner. Whatever you choose to use doesn't really matter. Just choose a planner that works for you. Use it, and stick with it. I've never forgotten that time is the stuff life is made of.

One of my athletic teams in high school shouted out this saying before each competition: "Do it! Do it right! Do it right now! Let's go Vikings!" Your chance to gain control of your time is always now. By living every day as if it is one of our last, we will empower ourselves to beat any personal obstacles standing in our way of success.

CHAPTER 5

The Power of Thinking BIG

"I believe that this nation should commit itself to achieving the goal, before this decade is out, of landing a man on the moon and returning him safely to the Earth."
— President John F. Kennedy, May 25, 1961

Some people regarded Kennedy's dream as lunacy. Others thought the President of the United States was crazy. How could we send a man to the moon, let alone land on it? The closest thing to this feat happened in 1957 when the Soviet Union sent the Sputnik satellite into orbit. That was just a satellite and its objective was merely getting into space!

He knew he was surrounded by doubt and skepticism, but Kennedy believed in his dream and didn't doubt it could be done. He went to work by meeting with Vice President Lyndon Johnson and his science advisors to come up with a plan. Kennedy led Congress in pursuit of this seemingly impossible mission. They took action after action and invested significant time, money and resources in this quest.

CNN writer Richard Stenger summarized the result: "Despite skeptics who thought it could not be accomplished, Kennedy's dream became a reality on July 20, 1969, when Apollo 11 commander Neil Armstrong took a small step for himself and a giant step for humanity, leaving a dusty trail of footprints on the moon."

The impossible became possible. President Kennedy's ability to think big gave Americans tremendous confidence and something we could share with the rest of the world. With a little more than five months to spare, America met Kennedy's end-of-the-decade goal. In the years that followed, more astronauts reached the lunar surface and soon it became a rather common accomplishment.

Without Kennedy's vision, and the goal he set that inspired the nation, how long would it have taken us to reach the moon? What "trips to the moon" would you like to take in your lifetime? Without a big idea, dream or aspiration, you'll never know what you are capable of. Your big idea will give you passion and add juice to your life.

AIM FOR THE STARS

Shortly after I graduated from dental school, I started a dental practice from scratch. I quickly discovered we hadn't learned much about business in dental school. So I decided to find some business mentors and coaches to help me leapfrog to success instead of trying to figure things out on my own, which can be costly.

One of my early mentors, Dr. Dick Barnes, taught me this principle: "It's better to aim for a star and barely miss, than it is to aim for a cow-pie and hit it dead center."

After all, what do you have to lose by thinking big? I couldn't see a reason not to aim for the stars, so I decided to do just that. I set big goals and headed out to reach them. This thinking allowed me to hit my break-even point earlier than many start-up businesses do.

Over time, I learned I wouldn't always reach my big goals. I also discovered it feels better to come close to a huge goal than it does to reach a mediocre goal without working for it. You'll feel a sense of excitement when you pursue a big goal. Your dream will often become a reality as passion meets action.

BIG THINKING PRODUCES BIGGER RESULTS

As a young businessman, I was hungry for wisdom. I had learned how to remove tooth decay, treat disease and beautify smiles through cosmetic dentistry. I had learned to diagnose and treat many conditions through oral health. What I hadn't yet developed was a good foundation in running a business. And if I couldn't stay in business, then I wouldn't be able to help people.

Early in my career, I went to Chicago to attend a seminar on business strategies for dentists. I met two doctors who were older than me and polar opposites of each other. One had a small practice that hadn't grown significantly over a period of many years. He said more than twenty years ago, his parents had bought the building for him and set him up with everything he needed. The business hadn't experienced significant growth since then.

The other doctor was an immigrant who'd sacrificed everything he had to get to the United States. He conquered many obstacles, learned to speak English and started out flat broke. None of it mattered—he had a big dream.

Today he is an extremely successful doctor and businessman, no doubt a multimillionaire, with something like nine dentists working for him! There's a saying…when the student is ready, the teacher will appear. I was ready and delighted to accept an invitation from Dr. Nalin Patel to join him for breakfast. I took notes and soaked up like a sponge everything he said.

Dr. Patel taught me one thing that stands out still today. He taught me the importance of thinking big. As we took the escalator from the restaurant to the seminar, he looked at the chandeliers and accompanying dÈcor of the great hotel. I wondered what he was doing. As big a success as I revered him already to be, he was thinking even bigger, much bigger. He was getting design ideas for his next multi-doctor dental building. He told me to pick up a copy of David J. Schwartz's book, The Magic of Thinking Big. I promptly did so and devoured it. I highly recommend this book to you and anyone who wants to see big progress.

THE MAGIC OF BIG THINKING

The message of David J. Schwartz's book is simple, yet empowering. There are many elements to the results derived from big thinking. As I reflect upon what remained with me most, I'm amazed at how big results are easier to come by than I ever thought possible. This thing called the mind is a very powerful asset. I learned it often takes no more effort to accomplish a BIG goal than it does to reach a mediocre one. In other words, many times it requires the same effort to accomplish something small as it does to accomplish something huge. Even crazier still, sometimes it takes more effort to reach small goals.

Big thinkers enjoy many advantages over mediocre thinkers. Amazing things happen when you know exactly what you want and are passionate about it. So keep going. When you visualize your goal, think about it all the time and take continuous action toward it, you'll see incredible results. That which is necessary to accomplish your big goal tends to fall into place. The elements of the "how" have a tendency to align themselves, often with no great effort on your part. Enthusiasm is born and grows. It's almost like throwing fuel on the fire. Your attention, focus, and energy toward your objective will multiply. As T. Harv Eker says, "Where attention goes, energy flows—and the results show!" It's so much fun, it doesn't even feel like work. You could just go on doing it all day long, every day and not get tired of it.

WHY THE MASSES REMAIN IN MEDIOCRITY

I've read study after study with the same results. We all want to succeed. Back in the early fifties, Earl Nightingale said this about the level of wealth in America: "In America right now, there are more than 25 million people 65 years of age and older. Most of them are broke; they're dependent on someone else for life's necessities."

Today isn't much different. I've read countless books, articles, studies and reports. I've listened to live and recorded speeches from experts in personal development and motivation. I've even found the same results in my own industry. The American Dental Association reports that at retirement age, up to ninety-five percent of American dentists cannot retire and maintain their current lifestyle. More people in all industries have to work well beyond retirement age just to survive.

Yes, we all want to succeed. We'd all love to accomplish our big goals...and I'm talking about more than just financial goals. Yet the majority of people fail and never accomplish their goals or live their dreams. Why? Rollo May, a distinguished psychiatrist, sheds great light on this subject. In his book, Man's Search for Himself, he said, "The opposite of courage in our society is not cowardice...it is conformity."

Earl Nightingale said the problem with conformity is people act like everyone else without knowing why or where they are going. All too often, it's easier to settle for mediocrity because everybody else does. We admire people for being very successful and wonder why we can't be like them. The good news is—we can! Successful people put their pants on one leg at a time, just like everybody else. The difference is they don't settle for mediocrity, and they don't accept less than the very best from themselves. They aren't afraid to step off the beaten path just because nobody else will. I'm going to conclude this thought with a portion of the Robert Frost poem, "The Road Not Taken."

Two roads diverged in a yellow wood, and I—
I took the one less traveled by,
And that has made all the difference.

THE FASTEST MILE

"The man who can drive himself further once the effort
gets painful is the man who will win."
— Roger Bannister

Back in the early fifties, the worlds of sports and medicine agreed it was physically impossible for anyone to run the mile in under four minutes. Some experts believed the human heart would give out under such conditions. One person, the great Roger Bannister, didn't believe any of it. He knew it was a myth and set out to dispel it.

Bannister had just come off a dismal loss in the 1952 Olympics. He was extremely disappointed with his fourth place finish and failure to win a medal. So he set out to accomplish a new goal, a big goal. He was going to become the first person ever to run the mile in under four minutes. The training began. He ignored the naysayers and went to work. He chose some of the fastest runners to be his pacers as he ran each lap.

He had a vision and kept at it until the big day: May 6, 1954. In a packed stadium at Oxford University, Bannister ran the race of his life. The announcer started to read Bannister's first-place time of "three minutes and…" but the roar of the crowd drowned out the rest. Roger Bannister had achieved what had been proclaimed impossible. His record-shattering time for running the mile? It was 3:59.4—that's 3 minutes, 59.4 seconds.

Shortly thereafter, several others accomplished the same feat, and it's common with runners today. What happened? Did people suddenly become physically superior to all those who had run before 1954? Did miraculous medical advancements make it possible for others to follow Bannister's lead and break the four-minute mile barrier? No way. All that happened was one person wasn't afraid to aim high and expect more. The big barrier up to then had been a mental one. Once people knew a four-minute mile was possible, they believed and set out to accomplish it.

Is there a four-minute mile you'd like to run? What seemingly impossible task can you set out to do today? I'd like to make a suggestion. From now on, anytime the word "impossible" pops into your head, replace it with "*I'm* possible!" and go for it! You'll never know how good you can be until you aim high and go for it.

SUMMARY

I hope you're feeling rejuvenated and full of enthusiasm for life. Your new beginning starts today—and *every* day! As you move forward, your big thinking and desire for a better life will take you far. You'll be surprised when you discover how good you are. When you surprise yourself, remember you've always been capable of achieving your big dreams. Believe in yourself, aim for the stars and realize your possibilities are literally limitless!

SECTION TWO

IMPLEMENT

CHAPTER 6

Experience the Law of AttrACTION

"The greatest discovery of my generation is that human beings can alter their lives by altering their attitudes of mind."
— William James

A few years ago, one of my employees received a book, *The Secret*, as a gift from her mother. She said she'd read it, but didn't like it. She dismissed it as mostly a bunch of nonsense. She gave it to me, since she knew I was "into all that positive thinking stuff."

I'd become familiar with what many call the "Law of Attraction" before Rhonda Byrne made it popular with the book and movie. I was glad to accept the book from my employee and enjoyed reading it. It is an informative book and provides powerful insight into a natural law that many experts believe governs the universe.

Though I believe the Law of Attraction does exist and work, I also firmly believe in a loving God who cares about all of us. God provides a way for us to accomplish what He expects of us and the goals He inspires us to pursue. I believe the earth, along with many important and powerful laws of nature—including the Law of Attraction—was created for all of us.

Let me tell you how I interpret the Law of Attraction. We become what we think about, good or bad. We tend to get what we think about, both on the conscious and subconscious levels. We bring into our lives what we think about most, especially when our thoughts are accompanied by positive emotion. Powerful author and motivational speaker T. Harv Eker has great insight into this in what he calls the "Law of Manifestation."

$$T \Rightarrow F \Rightarrow A \Rightarrow R$$

We all have thoughts, some are good and some are bad. The thoughts we hold in our minds lead to the feelings we have. Our feelings lead to the actions we take. Finally, the actions we take produce the results we get. I have found this model to be true in my life. It's just like the law of the harvest: We sow what we reap, and we reap what we sow. That's why it's so incredibly important which thoughts we allow to stay in our minds.

THOUGHTS BECOME THINGS

If you think about it long and hard enough, you'll realize that every action you've ever taken started as a thought. We don't do anything silly or regrettable without first having some sort of thought about taking that action. Conversely, we never do anything noteworthy or great without first thinking about it. Thoughts eventually become things. We have to control our thoughts if we want to be happy in life. Our minds are constantly bombarded with information, images, music, ideas and messages. Some are constructive, but many are destructive. Happy is the person who can control his own thoughts!

Your mind is like a stage. There's always something or someone on stage seeking your attention. When a non-supportive or negative thought makes its way to the stage, it's your job to pull the curtain until you can replace that negative or annoying thought with something constructive. The more you can control your thoughts, the greater your chances of success. I suggest you always have some sort of uplifting song, memory or past success in the back of your mind to toss on your mind's stage in the moments of doubt, fear or negativity. Doubt and fear never accomplish anything positive—and they never will.

In Good Company

Over the years, I've studied the philosophies and lives of many successful people. It's been quite fascinating because I've discovered a definite pattern in how they make it to success. Without question, each knew about the Law of Attraction in some form or another, whether or not he or she called it that. It has been around for centuries.

In my opinion, the biggest element of this law is *faith in the unseen*. It requires you to believe in a power much greater than yourself. When you set your sights on a big objective, it's important to put your trust in a Higher Power because, remember, you can't do it alone. My Higher Power is an all-knowing God. So many of my mentors and role models have given similar descriptions of their experiences with the Law of Attraction. An unseen force brings into our lives the people, things, circumstances, events or ideas to make our dominant thoughts a reality. Thoughts on both our conscious and subconscious levels apply equally to this law.

EMOTION INTENSIFIES THE RESULTS

Looking at the speed and depth of the Law of Attraction, emotion seems to play the most important part of all in the process. Our thoughts and desires become many times more powerful when we let them out and give them validity through our emotions. Emotions of excitement, enthusiasm, love and gratitude are among the most powerful for us to tap into. Emotions of fear, doubt, revenge and hate bring the most destruction and slow our progress tremendously. Your positive emotions, coupled with your positive thoughts and desires, bring synergistic results. Bear in mind that the converse is also true. Negative emotions, coupled with your negative thoughts, will attract more of what makes you feel bad—and more of what you *don't* want.

By now you probably realize how important it is to feel good and—no matter what—find what works best for you to maintain positive thoughts. Doing noble things that make you feel good will have a great impact in attracting good and positive changes to your life. It's important to stay focused on feeling as good as you can as often as you can.

WHAT GOES AROUND, COMES AROUND

Another way of looking at the Law of Attraction is to consider the path of a boomerang. Throw the boomerang out and before long it comes flying right back to you. We all throw boomerangs every day of our lives, whether we know it or not. Some boomerangs are good and some are bad. Some of the best boomerangs we can throw are acts of kindness, love and service toward others. Looking out for the interests of others is one of the best things we can do for ourselves.

Zig Ziglar explains it this way, "You can have everything in life you want if you will just help enough other people get what they want."

Some of the worst boomerangs we throw are complaining, justifying and blaming. Anytime you catch yourself in one of these three actions, watch out. These actions attract negativity perhaps faster than anything else. Think for a moment about times when things weren't going well in your life. There's a good chance you'd complained, justified or blamed something or someone for your circumstances.

The mindset we choose to feed is so important. We can choose to have an abundance mentality, or we can choose to have a scarcity mentality. Those with a scarcity mentality tend to hoard their money, time, talents and resources. They live in fear there won't ever be enough good to go around. On the other hand, those with an abundance mindset are just the opposite. They readily share their money, time, talents and resources with others. They live in abundance and know there's more than enough to go around.

Thomas S. Monson recently taught that scarcity and abundance exist simultaneously. Think about that for a moment! Depending on your mindset, you can choose abundance or you can choose scarcity. It's your choice. I know which I choose. The only thing I can advise here is always to think abundance. Focus on abundance and be amazed!

PUTTING THE LAW TO WORK FOR YOU

Much has been written and many people speak about the Law of Attraction. My understanding of it is getting better day-by-day. I don't claim to be an expert in putting this law to work. However, I do know who was an expert on the subject before it became part of popular culture. It was Napoleon Hill. His book, *Think and Grow Rich*, is the best I've read about the Law of Attraction. Though I don't share Hill's religious views in his book, I do think the book has many great ideas and insights.

Bob Proctor and Dr. Joe Vitale are also experts on the Law of Attraction. I suggest you study their materials if you want to get a better grip on how this law can work for you. I learned the most important aspect in seeing the Law of Attraction at work from successful stock market investor Natalie Pace. I had the privilege to hear Natalie speak at a seminar a few years ago. She said the Law of Attraction is really the Law of AttrACTION. It works best when we take lots of action.

Joe Vitale has said it works even better with *inspired* action—to the point where your actions almost feel effortless. It's fun to see the Law of Attraction work to your benefit!

SUMMARY

If you want to improve your life, you'll do it much faster by properly implementing the Law of Attraction. Mind you, this law is not a replacement for good old-fashioned work. When the law is working, however, the "work" you do will not be drudgery. It will be an enjoyable, seemingly effortless way to pass time that could normally continue on all day long. Using this law takes practice and your firm belief that as you do your best and do what's right, all things will work together for your own good. If your good results haven't arrived yet, believe and know they're on the way because they surely are.

CHAPTER 7

Achieve More With Goals

"If you're bored with your life—if you don't get up every morning with a burning desire to do things—then you don't have enough goals."
— Lou Holtz

Much of what we've covered involves goals. My thoughts and ideas about goals have been shaped by many of my mentors over the years. I'd like to credit Zig Ziglar, Brian Tracy and Bill Bartmann for helping me understand how to set and reach big goals. I am astonished when I read studies that show the large number of people who don't set goals. And, according to Brian Tracy, ninety-seven percent of the people who say they've set goals never actually put them in writing.

What is a goal anyway? A goal is a declaration of something you want to accomplish in the future. People who want to improve in life will undoubtedly set and achieve many goals. They will be relentless and persistent in their pursuit, regardless of obstacles that might get in the way.

I love the advice Bill Bartmann gives to people who want to set goals. He says to call them "promises" instead of "goals." He shares data from some Harvard studies. About seventy percent of goals people set are reached. However, people keep more than ninety-five percent of their promises. People in general really want to keep their promises.

PUT YOUR GOALS IN WRITING

In my opinion, Brian Tracy is one of the most qualified people to teach about setting goals and how to accomplish them. Over his career, he has helped millions of people effectively set and achieve goals. As mentioned previously, ninety-seven percent of people who make goals never put them in writing. What does that mean? If you put goals in writing, you'll put yourself in the top three percent of goal-setters! The odds of reaching your goal—or keeping your promise—go way up if you put it in writing. You can do that. Everyone can. There's really no reason, from now on, to keep you from writing down your goals.

Once you've put your goals in writing, it's important to put them in places you see daily. Looking at your goals, will cause you to think about them more. Since you become what you think about, you'll greatly increase your chances of keeping your promises—your goals—if you see them often.

In addition to written goals, it's powerful to record your goals on a tape or CD. Put the CD in your car or MP3 player. Then listen to your goals and promises when you're commuting or have any down time. Hearing them in your own voice will help you focus on ways to accomplish them.

SUCCESSFUL GOAL FORMAT

I love Brian Tracy's three-step format for setting any goal. The first step is to write your goal in the present tense. Second is always to use positive words and phrases such as "I can" or "I am." Avoid phrases such as, "I will quit." For example, instead of saying, "I will quit smoking," say "I am smoke free by such-and-such date." Third is to personalize your goal. Always use the word "I" followed by some sort of action. This signals your subconscious mind. With goals, simpler and shorter is better. For example, "I earn $20,000 a month by June 1, 2010."

CRITICAL STEPS FOR GOAL-SETTING

To set any goal properly, you must follow certain steps. Zig Ziglar, Brian Tracy, Bill Bartman and James Malinchak teach a similar method for goal setting. By following these six steps, you're more likely to reach your goals and keep your promises. You'll be on top of your game and overcome the obstacles that would otherwise hold you back.

The first, and most important, step is to identify your goal and set a deadline for its completion. Please make sure it is YOUR goal and not that of somebody else. All too often we think we have to accomplish or chase dreams other people have for us. If it is your goal and you are passionate about it, you will more easily work toward fulfilling it. This is time to declare your goal, using the successful goal format described above. Here's the goal I wrote for this book: "I am the author of *Beating All Odds*, and I have the published book in my hands by June 1, 2009."

The second step is to identify the rewards related to reaching your goal. Why work toward this goal? What will you get when you accomplish it? The more excited you are about the benefits, the more passionate you'll be about reaching your goal. I listed several benefits for writing this book: "I will leave a legacy for my children. I will have increased self-confidence and expand my professional network. The book will provide me with another income stream. The book will serve as a powerful lead-generating tool for future business. Most important, I hope my book will inspire people in a time where many are losing hope."

The third step is to identify the knowledge and skills you need to accomplish your objective. There were several keys to writing this book. I needed the self-discipline to invest at least two hours every day, Monday through Saturday, for a set period of time. I needed to learn how to categorize my computer documents into a book folder. I needed to properly spell-check each document.

The fourth step is to identify the main obstacles that could keep you from accomplishing your goal. For me, the main obstacle was finding time to write this book, all while being a good husband and father of six children, running four businesses and actively serving my church and community…among other things! Meeting deadlines is the biggest dragon to slay. But without those deadlines, I couldn't get anything done!

The fifth step is to identify people who can help you reach your goal. Now, I could have tried on my own to figure out how to write and publish a book. Or I could leapfrog my way to success by benefiting from the experience of an expert. I'm a little lazy here. I'm not interested in working any harder than I have to! So I hired a publishing coach to hold me accountable for each step of the book-writing process. My coach is an international bestselling author who walks the walk and talks the talk. You don't want to take advice from someone unless that person has "been there and done that." So I used my coach's recommended network of editors, proofreaders, publishing professionals, etc.

The sixth step is to create a unique plan of action to reach your goal. My plan: "For a period of three months, I will focus all day on writing my book. I plan to work intensely for at least two hours daily, except Sundays, for as long as it takes to finish the book. Most importantly, I need to do what my publishing coach says, by the given deadlines."

BALANCE YOUR GOALS FOR A BALANCED LIFE

Setting and achieving goals is a rewarding experience. However, if we have too many financial and career goals, and not enough family or physical goals, our lives will be out of balance. We need to have goals in several major categories. I like the way Zig Ziglar teaches the need to balance life's priorities. He illustrates the idea with a wheel that has seven spokes. If each spoke is the same length, the ride will be smooth. However, if the spokes are different lengths, then the ride will be bumpy! Ziglar's seven major "spokes," or goal categories, are career, social, financial, family, physical, mental and spiritual. The bigger the goals, the longer the spokes. With longer spokes, each revolution of the wheel results in much more progress.

Don't be afraid to set big goals and make big promises to yourself. When you push yourself to step outside your comfort zone, you'll gain experience and you'll grow. Accomplishing big goals is fun and key to your success. However, I firmly believe that what we become from reaching our goals is far more important than what we get.

REWARD YOURSELF FOR YOUR SUCCESS

Remember one of the most important parts of reaching any goal. Celebrate! Reward yourself with something special. Make a big deal about your successes. Doing so builds positive momentum that will carry you onto your next goals. It also burns that feeling of empowerment deeper into your memory. These powerful memories will drive away discouragement when it rears its ugly head in the future.

SUMMARY

There's a big difference between those who don't have goals and those who do. The data overwhelmingly indicates that goal setters and achievers have much higher incomes than those who don't. Along with that comes a greater sense of fulfillment, happiness, confidence and hope for a better future.

Choose today to be in the top three percent. Set your goals properly, write them down and take continuous action until you've reached—or exceeded—those goals. You'll reap the rewards that flow to those who know where they're going and how they're going to get there.

CHAPTER 8

Plan Your Work

"Have a plan. Follow the plan, and you'll be surprised how successful you can be. Most people don't have a plan. That's why it is easy to beat most folks."
— Paul "Bear" Bryant

Back in 1992, I learned a simple, yet powerful, concept that has remained with me and helped me many times during my career. It's as simple as this: Plan every day the night before.

Since then, I've had this concept reinforced by the greatest speakers and experts in time management. Some call it the "power hour." But it should only take ten minutes a day to make this strategy work for you. All you need to do is sit down with your day planner; think about the day ahead and devise a strategy to make that day count. Your goal should be to maximize your productivity and give yourself every chance to control the day instead of letting your day control you. By deciding in advance what you want to accomplish and setting a plan to achieve it, you can go into your day with laser beam focus. Like a laser beam, you can slice through the distractions and noise that would hold you back and slow your productivity.

USE A PLANNER

The most successful people I know use a day planner. There have been times when I've used a planner and times when I've not used a planner. There's a staggering difference in accomplishment and productivity between the two. There are many different planners and time management systems available. It's not critical which planner or system you choose, as long as you pick one that's right for you and use it daily.

I've used several time management planners in my life and finally found my favorite. It's called The Performance Planner ™ and was developed by Zig Ziglar. You can learn more about it at www. ziglartraining.com. The Performance Planner is a comprehensive personal management and goals achievement system. It is user friendly, effective and inexpensive.

With my planner, I can quickly review the day's events and track how I've done toward achieving my daily goals. I can easily monitor the progress I've made and see where I need to improve. Achievement experts agree that the best way to improve performance is to measure it. You'll find using a planner allows you easily to track whatever you want in life. Is there any aspect of your life, career or business you would like to improve? Then track your progress in that area on a daily basis. Using your planner will help you remain focused. Where the focus goes, the energy flows and the results show!

Recently I went back several months in my planner and reviewed the progress I'd made. It reminded me again about the importance of time management.

"Time management is the art or act of controlling events."
— Hyrum Smith

I found several stretches during that two-month period where my days were blank. Then there were stretches where my days were packed full of completed tasks, highlighted areas and notes in the margins about objectives I'd accomplished. It's no mystery that the major progress and productive breakthroughs came most often on days I stuck to my plan. On days I didn't have a plan, I was controlled by those ever-present random events.

Using a day planner to plan your work and then sticking to that plan will help you reach your goals much quicker. You can become a master of time management. By mastering the principles of time management, you control your daily events. The old adage is true: If you fail to plan, you plan to fail. It's that simple. When you don't plan your days, by default, the random events of the day will control you.

KILL THE TIME VAMPIRES

We're all subject to the destructive effects time vampires can have on us if we don't recognize and kill them. What is a time vampire? It is anything that steals your focus and diverts your attention and energy from what's most important. A time vampire could be the phone, e-mail, text messages, problems or tasks that could—and should—be handled by your assistants (if you have them). Other time vampires include mindlessly watching TV, surfing the net, opening the mail, unscheduled solicitations and the list goes on.

E-mail can be a double-edged sword. It is an incredibly effective way to communicate with people around the world. Sending a message to a large group just by clicking a button allows you to accomplish what used to take hours, even days, by mail or telephone. This technology is amazing—when used properly. However, it can distract you and interrupt your productivity. Let me explain. If you spend the day checking your e-mail, then your focus will shift and bounce all over the place. Any momentum you have built for important tasks can be lost in a matter of minutes. Most e-mail messages are not as important as your highest priorities for the day. You may think you need to answer your e-mail right away. Then before you know it, you're out of time and you've failed to accomplish what you'd set out to do that day.

I suggest you check your e-mail once or twice a day. Of course, there are job-related exceptions to this. Limiting the number of times you check your e-mail allows you to focus on your priority tasks. Priority tasks give the greatest return on your investment of time. Identify when you are most productive and use those blocks of time to focus on your priority tasks.

Identify what time vampires are specific to your life and develop a plan to avoid them. Decide what you want to accomplish during the day and know what distractions may pop up. Then you will be more likely to maintain your focus and dodge those vampires that would divert you and steal your time.

CHOOSING YOUR TOP FOUR

Have you ever made a list of everything you need to accomplish during the day, only to discover a seemingly endless number of tasks to do? For me, it tends to happen more often than not. Experts in human achievement agree that it's better to accomplish fewer, but more meaningful, things during the day than it is to get a lot done that has little impact on the big picture. Less is often more.

List what you want to achieve during the day; then immediately identify the top four most important tasks on that list. These things are your highest return on investment activities and most important in helping you come closer to achieving your big goals. If you focus on these four things during any available time and work with intensity to complete them, you'll be amazed at the cumulative results as the days go on. You'll reach your big goals much faster than you imagined! The funny thing is, all those other things have a way of getting done—or disappearing—in the process.

PLAN AT LEAST ONE KEY ACTION

Think about your life's purpose, your biggest dreams, your biggest goals. Every day, plan at least one action to take you toward your major objective in life. If you plan to do at least *something* that relates to your big goal, you will be surprised at how much faster you will be able to achieve what might have seemed impossible. Always stay focused on the amount of progress you'll make if you just take daily and consistent action toward fulfilling your dreams.

SCHEDULE TIME TO THINK

In the hustle and bustle of your busy day, it's easy to go from one thing to the next all day. Keith Cunningham, entrepreneur and business coach, taught me that thinking is one of the most important and productive activities any of us can do. He taught me to remember to schedule time to think. This is time where you are alone and away from distractions. It can be a mere ten minutes or even thirty minutes. Some of our biggest personal breakthroughs, inspirations and answers to life's problems often come when we take the time to think and ponder what's most important to us.

If you don't do this on a regular basis, you are in for a real treat. Before you let another day go by, schedule time *today* to get away from the phone, e-mail, office, whatever, and just think. Think about your goals and the challenges you face. Examine them from all possible angles. I think you'll be pleasantly surprised to find quantum leaps in progress as your thinking time evolves. You'll also find an element of recharging and rejuvenating along the way.

Summary

Life is all about time. How would you like to have an extra day or two each month to do whatever you want? You could take extra vacation days. You could spend more time with your family. You could devote more time to that project you've wanted to finish. You could go fishing. You could be free to do anything you feel would enrich and enhance your quality of life.

I have great news. It's entirely possible—and it's within *your* power! You already know what I'm going to say. However, let me remind you of our earlier discussion. If you get better at planning your work, your play and your life, and then implement those plans, you'll save an hour here and an hour there. Added up, you'll probably give yourself that extra day at the end of the month. You'll have more time to do whatever you choose. Proper planning yields control over your time. Those who have control over their time greatly increase their chances of beating their odds.

CHAPTER 9

Work Your Plan

"Can anything be sadder than work left unfinished?
Yes; work never begun."
— Christina Rossetti

As we've just discussed, the best time to plan the next day's events is the night before. By then, you've had a chance to think about the upcoming day from all angles and you'll be able to form an effective strategy. You'll fall asleep with your plans and objectives for the day alive in your subconscious.

We've talked about programming your mind for success. Your subconscious mind is most receptive in the twenty minutes just before bed and twenty minutes immediately after you rise in the morning. During those times, make sure to feed your mind with positive, inspiring and uplifting material. This is absolutely critical. Your subconscious mind never sleeps. It works around the clock. Often, while you are asleep, your subconscious mind is working on ways to carry out your plans. So before you go to bed, make sure to use the last twenty minutes in a constructive way by filling your mind with positive and uplifting thoughts, sounds and images.

What should you allow to enter your mind during those twenty minutes? Read, listen to, or think about what inspires you and what makes you feel good. Focusing on pleasant things that draw out positive emotions maximizes the good your subconscious mind can do. Reading good books is one of the easiest and best things to do to put yourself in the right mindset. Another great thing to do is to focus on all the many things you're thankful for. We'll talk about gratitude in another chapter.

What about the negative stuff? We've already talked about how watching the news is one of the worst things to do before going to bed. Why? Negative news sells, so more often than not, negative news is what we get. We give away our power when we let in the negative, especially right before we go to bed. The depressing, negative, gloomy, fearful thoughts and feelings elicited by the news stay with our subconscious all night and the effects can be destructive. With that in mind, it's also important not to fall asleep listening to the radio. Again, doing so allows us to give away all our control. We run the risk that negative lyrics, messages and stories will affect our subconscious mind.

After you rise in the morning and get yourself off to that positive start, it's time to begin working your plan. Here we go! Time to roll up your sleeves and get after it. Are you ready? Take a moment to review your plans for the day and how you see the day unfolding. Having daily goals and then visualizing them greatly increases your chances of carrying out your plans. Be grateful for a brand-new day that's all yours.

GETTING STARTED

Here comes the hard part. Have you ever started the day in a bad mood? You're up and at it, but you just don't feel like going after it all. And you don't even come *close* to feeling like going to work. Ever felt that way? I know I have and so has everybody else. What should you do when this happens? Get started—whether you feel like it or not! In fact, do it *especially* if you don't feel like it. Something magic will happen.

Eventually you will feel like going after it, and you'll gather momentum along the way.

Here's the good news. Those who force themselves to do the things they need to do, when they need to do them, will eventually be able to do the things they want to do, when they want to do them. Remember, everybody struggles with being up, on and in the mood all the time. The people who regularly beat their odds are the ones who can get themselves moving, especially when they don't feel like it. It's been said by many before me that you'll get a lot more done through movement than you will by meditation!

Where do we start each day? I love what Brian Tracy teaches in his book, *Eat That Frog*. He uses a great analogy to drive home a point. I learned this principle from my mother years before I read Tracy's book. She taught me to do the unpleasant task first. Successful people understand the wisdom behind this. As Tracy points out, if you have to eat a frog, that frog will not get any prettier if you just stare at it or think about it. So just eat it and be done with it. If we go through our day with that frog staring at us, it often appears to get bigger and uglier with each passing hour. Getting the frog out of the way early gives us confidence, builds momentum and enables us to move onto other important things. Try this. You'll be amazed at how much more effective your days will be.

LEARN TO PROCRASTINATE

Years ago, I was reading a book by one of my favorite authors, Robert Allen. He is an expert in personal development and creating wealth. In one chapter of the book, Allen gives readers the charge to learn to procrastinate. What? Are you kidding me? That's all I could think when I first read it. Up to that point in my life, I'd tried to avoid procrastination like the plague. Now somebody I trusted and admired was telling me to do it?

There will be tasks of little importance that can be put off, maybe indefinitely. As we discussed in the previous chapter, we need to focus on our top four priorities for the day and keep going until they are complete. Meanwhile, we can procrastinate on the less important items.

You may ask, "How long can I procrastinate on these things?" Perhaps forever. If they're important enough, then eventually they'll be delegated to someone else or rise on your priority list at a subsequent time. Many times they'll end up being dropped from your "To Do" list altogether with little or no consequence.

WORK: THERE IS NO SUBSTITUTE

Have you ever stood in awe of the amazing accomplishments of somebody you know personally? What allows them to overachieve and get such magnificent results? Often the answer is that successful people know how to work hard and stay at it until they get the outcome they seek. My older brother, Greg, is a perfect example of this trait, one of the most important personal components of beating the odds. Greg understands that good old-fashioned work will bring results like little else will.

When we were kids, Greg was always good at sports. When Greg was a high school senior, he was an excellent football player. He was a little too big to be a wide receiver and not quite big enough to be your ideal tight end. He was what many football experts call a "tweener," something in between. He had a great senior year and accomplished much. However, not many colleges were interested in giving him a football scholarship out of high school. He, however, did get a good scholarship to attend a nearby junior college.

Greg headed off to Ricks College in Rexburg, Idaho and was red-shirted his freshman year. He learned how to hit the weights hard, how to eat and how to practice. Then he left school for two years to serve as a church missionary. When he came back, he picked up right where he'd left off. He lifted weights, worked hard in practice and disciplined himself to do what it took to become a great football player. Goodbye tweener! Greg gained the weight, strength and speed he needed to become the Junior College All-American tight end. After his sophomore year, he was heavily recruited by many major universities, and chose Stanford University after being recruited by the legendary Bill Walsh.

Greg had two very successful seasons at Stanford and was invited to the NFL Scouting Combine, which provides an opportunity for the best college football players to perform physical and mental tests in front of NFL coaches, general managers and scouts. In essence, it's a five-day job interview. Greg must have made a great impression on some important people because the San Francisco 49ers traded up in the draft so they could select him as the seventy-eighth overall pick. Wow! My brother, who wasn't even picked for first team All-State in high school and was overlooked by all the big schools, was now headed to the NFL.

Greg picked up the Walsh's West Coast Offense quickly and made an immediate impact with the 49ers during his rookie year. He soon took the starting tight end position and had a great career in the NFL. I remember that great NFC wildcard playoff game in San Francisco against Brett Favre and the Green Bay Packers. If you are a football fan, you probably remember it too. Quarterback Steve Young threw a forty-three yard pass to receiver Terrell Owens to win the game at the end. Want to know who was named player of the game? It wasn't T.O.—it was Greg Clark! Greg had caught two touchdown passes and had an excellent game, making it possible for the 49ers to come back at the end for the win.

That was my own brother on national television on a regular basis. How cool is that? I remember John Madden, the well-known NFL commentator, rave about tight end Greg Clark. Steve Young called Greg Clark the best blocking tight end in football. I remember his NFL salary and bonuses. Greg decided to leave the NFL after five years due to repeated injuries.

Recently, I asked Greg how he'd been so successful with his football career. He explained that there really wasn't a secret to it. He just worked really hard and kept at it. He says people try to complicate things too much. When all's said and done, it usually comes down to good hard work. He did what he could do—and he did it very well. He worked long and hard. Sure, many others were perhaps more talented than he was. But, I doubt many knew how to work as hard as Greg. Then Greg reminded me about where he'd obtained his work ethic: the same place I did.

A & Z PRODUCE COMPANY

Greg and I, along with our five brothers, were fortunate because when we were young, our father and grandfather taught us about hard work. A & Z Produce Company is the family produce business. It started with my Grandpa Cliff Clark. He taught my father, who then taught my brothers and me. The wholesale produce business is a physically demanding business, with lots of hard work.

The days start very early in the produce industry. For as long as I can remember, I got up around two o'clock in the morning and left for work. As kids, we started out by sharpening pencils, emptying garbage cans, bagging fruit, picking up trash from the parking lot and anything else my Dad wanted us to do. When we grew tall enough to handle a two-wheeler, we kept busy loading and unloading trucks. I still remember those boxes of carrots and the lettuce trucks, heavy stuff!

Good hard labor at the warehouse often went on for ten or twelve hours or more. When 6:30 a.m. rolled around, I was so tired. I learned that if I just kept moving and stayed active, I wouldn't feel so worn out and the time actually went faster. It took quite a bit of discipline to get up early and work those long hours of physical labor. Then going home, it took discipline to explain to friends that it was time for sleep when they were ready to go water skiing or something.

Looking back on that time inspires me to this day. Without a doubt, those years taught me how to work hard for sustained periods of time. It's the work ethic that carried my brother into the NFL. It carried me through the rigors of eight years of intense study. I look at what my six brothers and sister are doing today and I'm awed by their successes. Coincidence? No way. We weren't straight A students and none of us did much better than the national average on standardized tests such as the ACT and SAT. But we all know how to work. Those who can learn how to work hard will have a competitive advantage over others in the workplace.

SUMMARY

There you have it. Plan your work and then work your plan. Combined, those two strategies yield a synergistic result. You can't have one without the other and expect to beat the odds that stand in the way of bringing your dreams to pass. The great secret to success in any worthy endeavor is work. There is no substitute. Work. Work. Work. If you'll just go to work on your dreams even when you don't feel like it, it won't be long before your dreams will work on you. You'll get excited. You'll see results. You'll get the momentum. You'll be into your work and, more importantly, your work will be into you.

CHAPTER 10

It's A Cinch By The Inch

"Start by doing what's necessary; then do what's possible; and suddenly you are doing the impossible."
— St. Francis of Assisi

Something cool happens when you utilize "dead" time. Some of my greatest "Ah-hah!" moments take place when I'm jogging, doing the dishes, working in the yard or cleaning the house after the kids have gone to bed.

One of the programs I listen to most is Zig Ziglar's *How to Stay Motivated* series. I just clip on my iPod and put on my ear phones. Funny thing is, I can remember exactly where I was when I learned something profound from one of Zig's audio series. For example, early one morning, I listened as Zig said—for the umpteenth time—something important. But this time it really sank in. That morning, during my exercise time, Zig Ziglar taught me one of the greatest success principles of all: Greatness doesn't happen overnight. Most often it doesn't come easily and it takes a significant length of time. The principle he teaches is this: It's a cinch by the inch, by the mile it's a trial. What's he talking about here?

Have you ever faced an enormous task, but every time you thought about it, you wondered how you'd ever get it done? Sure you have. We've all been there. If you're setting out to climb a mountain, just one look at the entire mountain can be overwhelming. When you focus on how long or how hard the task will be, you can quickly become nervous, intimidated and even feel like giving up. However, if you'll just take baby steps, you'll find you can achieve virtually anything. On any journey, just keep the end in mind. It's much easier to succeed with the big things by breaking them down into little steps. Those large tasks are often so much easier when you take it inch by inch, instead of worrying about accomplishing the whole thing at once.

IT'S A MARATHON, NOT A SPRINT

As I look back on my four years of dental school, I have lots of fond memories. Those were some good times. Many of my colleagues in dentistry think I'm crazy for thinking this way, but it's not crazy to me. Early in dental school, a classmate taught me how to approach the long haul that lay ahead. One day, I was overwhelmed with reading assignments, tests to study for, lab projects to complete, imposing deadlines, family responsibilities and on and on.

Seeing how overwhelmed I was, my classmate made a very logical statement, and I will always remember it. She said, "Remember, dental school is a marathon—not a sprint." In that moment, I understood exactly what she meant. It sank in right away. I didn't have to worry about climbing the entire mountain that day. All I had to do was make sure to keep moving and making progress toward the end. The race to the finish line in a marathon seldom, if ever, requires a sprint. It reassured me to realize I didn't have to tire myself out with needless sprints.

With this in mind, my years in dental school were productive, enjoyable and memorable. I accomplished everything I needed to do, lived a balanced life and got to smell the roses along the way. It's no different for you or me now. Today, I'm just running a different marathon and climbing different mountains. By applying that same thought process, the accomplishments continue to happen. Sometimes I'm amazed at how predictable success in any endeavor becomes when you just keep going.

Just this week, I attended a mastermind group meeting with several business owners, investors and professionals. We viewed a speech by motivational speaker Les Brown. His accomplishments are remarkable. He had many failures in life before he made it to success. I recommend any of his books, motivational CDs and DVDs—they are truly inspirational and informative.

"You can't lose if you don't quit. You will win, if you don't quit."
— Les Brown

I was reminded again that success is achievable if you just keep moving; keep taking those steps and never quit. The little things really do add up and become big things. Take courage in what you are trying to accomplish. I echo the counsel of Les Brown. Just keep going; keep doing the best you can. Because eventually, you *will* get there. The rewards are often great to the weary traveler who just took one more step.

CLIMBING YOUR EVEREST

About eight years ago, I heard Joseph B. Wirthlin deliver a classic speech titled, "One Step After Another." He referenced an article from the *Deseret News* and one from *Time* magazine titled, "Blind to Failure," by Karl Greenfeld. I quote this story as told by Wirthlin:

> Recently, I read about Erik Weihenmayer, a 33-year-old man who dreamed of climbing Mount Everest, a feat that defies many of the world's most expert climbers. In fact, nearly 90 percent of those who attempt the climb never reach the summit. Temperatures sink lower than 30 degrees below zero. Besides extreme cold, 100-mile-per-hour winds, deadly crevasses and avalanches, the climber must overcome the challenges of high altitude, lack of oxygen, and perhaps unsanitary food and water. Since 1953, at least 165 climbers have died in the attempt to scale the 29,000-foot summit.

> In spite of the risks, hundreds line up each year to make the ascent, Erik among them. But there is an important difference between Erik and every other climber who had attempted to ascend before: Erik is totally blind.

When Erik was 13 years of age, he lost his sight as a result of a hereditary disease of the retina. Although he could no longer do many of the things he wanted to, he was determined not to waste his life feeling depressed and useless. He then began to stretch his limits.

At age 16, he discovered rock climbing. By feeling the face of the rock, he found handholds and footholds that allowed him to climb. Sixteen years later, he began his ascent up Mount Everest. The story of his climb, as you might imagine, was filled with many harrowing and life-threatening challenges. But Erik eventually scaled the south summit and took his place with those who had gone before him, one of the few to stand on top of the highest mountain on the face of the earth.

When asked how he did it, Erik said, 'I just kept thinking… keep your mind focused. Don't let all that doubt and fear and frustration sort of get in the way.' Then, most importantly, he said, 'Just take each day step by step.'

Yes, Erik conquered Everest by simply putting one foot in front of the other. And he continued to do this until he reached the top.

Like Erik, we may have obstacles that would hold us back. We may even make excuses why we can't do what we want to do. Perhaps when we are tempted to justify our own lack of achievement, we can remember Erik, who, in spite of having lost his sight, accomplished what many thought was impossible simply by continuing to put one foot in front of the other.

An old proverb states that a journey of a thousand miles begins with a single step.

Sometimes we make the process more complicated than we need to. We will never make a journey of a thousand miles by fretting about how long it will take or how hard it will be. We make the journey by taking each day step by step and then repeating it again and again until we reach our destination.

I love that story! I've read it many times to remind myself of the possibilities out there, despite any weakness I may have. Erik was blind, yet he was blind to failure. How? He understood it's a cinch by the inch. The impossible becomes possible when we consistently take the steps that we can take, never stopping, until we reach the top.

Where are you on your quest to climb *your* Mount Everest? How can you apply this simple lesson to gain courage, enthusiasm, energy and desire to reach the peak?

SUMMARY

I'm going to summarize this chapter with a thought from the great businessman, philanthropist and author W. Clement Stone:

"Big doors swing on little hinges."

As you pursue your dreams, always remember that the little things make a big difference. Little actions, repeatedly taken, eventually yield big results. Visualize two big doors that open into a mansion. Then see, in your mind's eye, the little hinges that make it possible for those big doors to move. Never grow weary of doing the small things that often seem trivial or mundane. Keeping the big picture in mind while simultaneously moving forward is a sure way to succeed. The odds always favor those who remember that it's a cinch by the inch while it's often a trial by the mile.

SECTION THREE

PERSIST

CHAPTER 11

Persist Until You Succeed

"Success seems to be largely a matter of hanging on after others have let go."
— William Feather

"I will persist until I succeed." The most successful people I know live by this motto every day. This chapter is one of my favorites because it's where the rubber meets the road. It takes character to press forward after the initial excitement and emotion of setting a new goal wears off.

Real winners don't recognize failure, nor do they accept it as permanent. They see failure as just another stepping stone on the way to success. They know the difficulties and obstacles they face are all a part of the greater good set in their path to help them get to where they need to go.

THE RUDY RUETTIGER STORY

"It's always too soon to quit."
— Rudy Ruettiger

Many of you may not know who Daniel Ruettiger is, but you've probably seen the movie about his life. Remember the movie *Rudy*? Almost every time I ask that question, I get an affirmative response.

Many reply that *Rudy* is a classic inspirational movie—one of their all-time favorites. It's definitely one of my favorites. I've watched it multiple times and watch it again anytime I need some inspiration to keep after my dreams.

The movie is about a boy nicknamed Rudy who wanted to play football for the University of Notre Dame. But Rudy was small, not the typical type of player Notre Dame recruits, and he couldn't learn like the other kids. He had to work much harder than most just to get decent grades. His high school grades were nowhere near Notre Dame's standards. His family laughed at his ambitions, not just to get into Notre Dame, but to think he could join the Fighting Irish football team. They knew he would join his father and brothers at the local steel mill. That's exactly what he did for four years after high school. Then one day something inside him snapped. He went after his dream and wouldn't be denied for *any* reason. As Rudy recently told me, "It starts with something that's inside ya."

I'm fortunate to call Rudy one of my friends. We've had some great conversations. If you haven't seen the movie Rudy, get a copy and don't just watch it—memorize it! His story will inspire you and you'll be better because of it. As incredible as you'll find his Notre Dame football story, something even more inspiring took place for him after he left the University of Notre Dame.

PURSUING A NEW DREAM

I enjoy talking to Rudy about his life after his football days were over. He knew his Notre Dame success story—mostly what he went through to get there—needed to be told. The story would motivate millions and perhaps even save lives. So Rudy's drive to inspire people to overcome challenges and strive to be better was born. He decided to get Hollywood to make his story into a movie.

Several years passed as Rudy pursued his dream and pursued it hard—his life's goal and vision—of having a movie made about his life. He didn't know a soul in Hollywood, much less anyone with ties to the movie industry. But he wasn't going to let any of that stop him. He started where he was, did what he could, and—of course, he did his very best every moment of every day. Unfortunately, his contacts with Hollywood and Notre Dame…all ended in rejection. *NO. NO. NO!* No one thought the movie was a good idea.

When I asked Rudy about this, he said, "I guess that was their opinion. But my advice is: *Never* let anybody influence you or cause you to stop you from going after your dream. Pursue it with passion, keep pursuing it, and do whatever it takes to get it done!"

"You do what you can do and you do it really well." — Rudy Ruettiger

One day, Rudy was mowing the lawn at a complex where he worked when some people he'd thought were his friends drove by. He'd told them his dream of having his life story made into a movie. As they drove by with their windows down, they yelled at him and made fun of him, and said things such as, "Hey, Rudy, when you gonna get your movie made? Look at you! You're just cutting grass! What a loser!"

We've all been in similar situations, where someone scoffed at us or made fun of our goal or dream. Have you run into opposition that made you just want to quit? Have you worked so hard, for so long, only to feel like you hadn't made any progress at all? It's happened to us all. When you reach this point, you have two choices, and they're pretty simple: Either give in and quit—or don't. The choice is up to you, and only you. Never let anyone make that decision for you, because it's your dream.

Okay, let's get back to the story. Finally, Rudy couldn't take it anymore so he got angry. He quit his job in Indiana and went to the bank where he emptied out the small balance of his account. Then he bought an airline ticket and flew to Hollywood to go after his dream. Can you imagine? A "nobody" from Indiana was going to go door to door in Hollywood because nobody answered his phone calls or responded to his letters! Just think about it! Imagine the odds you'd face if *you* went to Hollywood and tried to convince someone to make a movie about *your* life. Well, Rudy faced those same big odds. He knew he had run out of options. So he did the only thing he knew to do; he kept moving forward, kept taking action. He didn't have anyone to tell him the proper way to get a movie made. Rudy knew every failed attempt just brought him closer to success. If the action didn't bring him closer to his goal, then he knew not to repeat it again.

Rudy spent eight years pursuing his dream and was rejected at every turn. I think most, if not all of us, would have given up by then—but not Rudy. He just kept going. Rudy believes that if the dream is big enough, then the obstacle doesn't matter. Finally, Rudy met a man whose brother knew Angelo Pizzo, writer and co-producer of the inspirational movie *Hoosiers*. Rudy arranged to meet with the writer, but Pizzo backed out. So Rudy called him. He was unsuccessful at first, so he kept at it—for more than two years! *No. No. No!* That's all he ever heard, until the day came when he finally received a response from Mr. Pizzo.

Pizzo told Rudy he wasn't going to make another sports movie because he didn't want to be labeled as a sportswriter. But because of Rudy's persistence, Pizzo finally agreed to have lunch with him under the condition that Rudy would leave him alone afterwards. Pizzo made it very clear that he was *not* interested in making Rudy's movie. Rudy agreed and they settled on a time to meet at a restaurant in Santa Monica.

You see, Rudy was convinced that if he could just have some time with the screenwriter, he would inspire and convince him to make the movie. Finally, after so many years of rejection, he was going to have a chance to be heard. Rudy was so excited; he arrived at the restaurant a few hours early. He could barely wait for Angelo Pizzo to arrive because then, Rudy knew, he would inspire him to make a movie about his life. Four hours later, Rudy still sat alone—because Pizzo never showed up. Time to quit? No way. Read on.

Rejected once again, Rudy left the restaurant with his head hanging low. Without really paying attention to his surroundings, he accidentally ran into a mail carrier. As dejected as he was, Rudy had a choice to make. He could either react and take out his frustrations on the mail carrier, or he could respond to the situation by being friendly. Fortunately, Rudy chose to respond by treating the mailman nicely. He apologized for running into him. A friendly conversation ensued and the mail carrier asked Rudy what had brought him all the way to California from Indiana. Painfully, Rudy explained he was there to have lunch with his friend, Mr. Pizzo, but he must have forgotten.

At that point, Rudy said, "Sir, it's been nice talking to you. Take care and I'll see you later." Then Rudy turned and began to walk down the street.

Suddenly the mail carrier yelled out, "Hey, Rudy! Do you mean Angelo Pizzo?"

Rudy turned back and responded, "Yeah! He's the one I was supposed to meet for lunch."

The mail carrier said, "Well, I know Angelo! I deliver his mail. His house is right over there."

Rudy said, "Oh, thank you!"

Then Rudy ran down the street and around the corner. He raced up to the front door of Mr. Pizzo's house and knocked on the door. Pizzo opened the door and said, "Who is it?"

Rudy's excitement bubbled out as he said, "It's Rudy!"

Surprised, Pizzo responded, "How did you find me?"

Rudy said, "It doesn't matter. You're late for lunch!"

Here's what Rudy told Mr. Pizzo in their conversation:

"Are you ready to make my movie? Because I'm not giving up. I don't care how many hoops I have to jump through. I want you to make the movie or put me in contact with somebody who will. I'm not doing this for money. I'm doing it because my story is going to change and save lives. I want you on board for this or the least you can do is connect me with somebody who believes in this purpose."

Just as Rudy thought, his story and persistence inspired Angelo Pizzo. Eventually Pizzo wrote and co-directed the award-winning movie *Rudy*. The movie has touched and inspired millions of lives, including my own.

Rudy says many people have told him his movie saved their children's lives, got them off drugs, inspired them to go to college, and more. And it continues, as the story is still alive today—all because one man with a dream refused to quit.

Today Rudy Ruettiger is a motivational speaker and corporate trainer who works with companies and organizations across the country. His web site is www.rudyinternational.com.

DON'T QUIT

Don't give up. Persist until you succeed. This is essential in all aspects of your life. During the tough times in life, those discouraging moments of temporary failure, I've often turned to a poem titled "Don't Quit." I've read it many times for inspiration and I want to share it with you.

Don't Quit

When things go wrong, as they sometimes will,
When the road you're treading seems all uphill,
When the funds are low and the debts are high,
And you want to smile, but you have to sigh,
When care is pressing you down a bit,
rest, if you must, but do not quit.

Life is queer with its twists and turns,
as every one of us sometimes learns.
And many a failure turns about
When he might have won had he stuck it out;
Don't give up, though the pace seems slow—
You might succeed with another blow.

Often the goal is nearer than
It seems to a faint and faltering man,
Often the struggler has given up
When he might have captured the victor's cup.
And he learned too late, when the night slipped down,
How close he was to the golden crown.

Success is failure turned inside out—
The silver tint of the clouds of doubt,
And you never can tell how close you are,
It may be near when it seems so far,
So stick to the fight when you're hardest hit—
It's when things seem worst that you must not quit.

— Author Unknown

In my own life, I've relied upon the power of persisting until I succeed. In so many instances, it seems everybody else gets off to a faster start than I do. It seems that so many people are smarter, more talented, don't have to work as hard, etc.

My Grandpa Clark, who has been extremely successful in life, reminds me repeatedly: "Slow and steady wins the race." We all know the story of the tortoise and the hare. The two race and the hare speeds out of sight as the tortoise plugs away. The hare gets distracted and makes some stops during the race. But not the tortoise. The tortoise persists and keeps going at his own pace. He does his best and eventually he crosses the finish line first.

On the way back from a family vacation several years ago, I was driving along the highway and spotted a billboard with a big picture of the great U.S. President Abraham Lincoln. Also on the billboard were these words: "Failed. Failed. Failed. And then....." Just below this quote were these words: "Persistence. Pass it on."

In Lincoln's case, that statement couldn't be more correct. Abraham Lincoln was considered a failure until he was well past age forty. Just imagine what the United States of America—and even the rest of the world—would have missed if Lincoln hadn't persisted. You must persist until you succeed.

HAVING THE WILLPOWER TO PERSIST

I love James Allen's classic book, *As a Man Thinketh*. It was published more than a hundred years ago, but to this day, it is one of the classic teachings about the power of the mind to create success. It is now available in the public domain—at no cost—and you'll find many sources on the Internet. You might not know it, but the book's title was based on a Bible verse from Proverbs 23:7: "As a man thinketh in his heart, so he is."

Allen concludes chapter two with a poem that sums up how I feel about persistence.

You will be what you will to be;
Let failure find its false content
In that poor word, "environment,"
But spirit scorns it, and is free.

It masters time, it conquers space;
It cows that boastful trickster, Chance,
And bids the tyrant Circumstance
Uncrown, and fill a servant's place.

The human Will, that force unseen,
The offspring of a deathless Soul,
Can hew a way to any goal,
Though walls of granite intervene.

Be not impatient in delay,
But wait as one who understands;
When spirit rises and commands,
The gods are ready to obey.

I hope you will stay focused on how much power you have as you persist until you succeed. Remember, you already have the willpower. Now just get started—put one foot in front of the other, and keep doing it, even when it seems to be a lost cause. Because you're never beaten until you quit.

The world owes a great debt to the great Thomas Edison. Among many things, Edison brought us incandescent electric light. Edison didn't succeed with his first attempt. In fact, he is famous for saying, "I have not failed; I've just found 10,000 ways that won't work." Edison knew that each failed attempt brought him a step closer to finding what *would* work. What if everyone had Edison's dedication to keep at it? Would your life be different if you had just kept at something a little longer? I've got a better question for you. How great will your life be from now on if you persist until you succeed?

SUMMARY

We will never know just how good we can be unless we cultivate the quality of persistence. Anybody who finds success in any endeavor must pass through many moments of temporary failure and seeming despair.

I'd like to conclude by sharing an experience of my own.

I was on the wrestling team in high school. I was an average athlete, nothing spectacular. My weight class was very competitive and I was always neck and neck with the number one guy on my team. I can't tell you how many times I lost to him by just one point or a few seconds. My goal was to beat him before high school was over. I knew I was one of the best wrestlers in the region, but I was hung up with this guy on my own team.

The last varsity challenge matches of the season arrived, and I had worked as hard, maybe harder, than anyone on the team. Finally, I had a chance to beat him. Well, it didn't happen. Another one-point loss to add to the pile. However, I ranked high enough in the region to make the sixteen-man bracket for the regional tournament. The top four wrestlers from the regional tournament would qualify for the state championships at BYU's Marriot Center in Provo, Utah.

The two-day regional tournament arrived. As luck would have it, my weight class included the returning state champion and one of the top four wrestlers in the state. I was up against one of those guys in my first match and lost by points. The odds were against me even making it to the state tournament, let alone having a chance to beating my high school nemesis. But I did the only thing I could do—I persisted. I'd persisted for five years and I wasn't going to quit then.

To make a long story short, I won four matches in a row. In my last match, I beat the guy who had just defeated the number one guy from my school—the guy I was never able to beat...or did I? I had just finished third in the region and was moving on to the state championships without him! I had defeated him. I just hadn't expected it would happen in that way. I'll never forget what my Coach Bart Thompson said, "A true champion gets up one time more than he is knocked down."

Persist until you succeed.

CHAPTER 12

Adversity,
the Greatest University

"If you can find a path with no obstacles,
it probably doesn't lead anywhere."
— Frank A. Clark

A few years ago, I heard a presentation by Ruben Gonzalez. It was very motivating because he focused on adversity, something we all face. Ruben's story is fascinating. He wanted to become an Olympic athlete, but wasn't sure which sport he'd most enjoy—and be competitive in. He wasn't very athletic and didn't stand out in any particular sport. He looked into each Olympic event to figure out where he'd have the best chance of doing well. Finally, Ruben made a choice. He chose the sport of luge.

Luge is grueling and dangerous. It involves speeding at up to seventy-five miles an hour, face up and feet first, in a special one-person fiberglass sled down an icy chute along a trail lined with more than a dozen perilous curves. The course is treacherous and being a slider (it's not called "luger," for some reason) is not many people's idea of a good time. In fact, many people told Ruben he was crazy and tried to discourage him from entering the hazardous sport. It wasn't long before Ruben learned that anyone who participates in luge ends up getting hurt, usually with broken bones. In fact, statistics show that nine out of ten people who take up the sport eventually give up and quit.

Discouraging? Ruben didn't see it that way. The difficulty, danger and high likelihood of injury actually excited him. He'd found a sport to compensate for his lack of athleticism, one where he could call upon one of his greatest strengths. You see, Ruben knew how to deal with setbacks. He knew he could handle the broken bones and push through adversity better than anyone. He knew he wouldn't quit. That alone gave him a big advantage over the competition.

After years of perseverance, broken bones and various setbacks, Ruben defied all odds when he qualified for the 2002 Salt Lake City Olympics at the ripe old age of thirty-nine. That age is almost unheard of for Olympians in any event, much less the grueling sport of luge. Ruben reached his dream because he mastered the art of plowing through—and benefiting from—adversity. Ironically, Ruben Gonzalez has been referred to as "The Rudy of Luge!"

Ruben says, "Your struggles make you stronger. Great people were not born great. They became great by having a dream, having the courage to take action and refusing to quit until they accomplished their dream. It's always, 'dream, struggle, victory.' If you're going through a struggle, don't quit! You're on the way to victory!"

TURNING FAILURE INTO SUCCESS

When I was a kid, my dad taught me a lesson I'll never forget. It has helped me countless times in my business life. Dad is a wholesale produce businessman and brings in fruits and vegetables from around the world to his business in Salt Lake City, Utah. He took a few of us kids with him on business trips from time to time. A hot spot for us was sunny California, where there was always plenty to do. Those trips were so much fun and it never felt like he was "working."

I remember one particular trip because of the lesson I learned from my dad. We were in the hotel room, and I heard him on the phone with one of his partners at the home office. A crisis of some sort was taking place and apparently he was walking them through it. After he hung up, he told my brother and me what was happening.

They had bought too many strawberries one week and the strawberries weren't selling as anticipated. They had hundreds, maybe even thousands of cases, to move. There's a saying in the industry: "You either sell it, or you smell it." Well, with the diminishing shelf life of this particular product, the home office was panicked at the possibility of losing its investment.

Then my dad explained his brilliant strategy. There was no trace of panic, worry or fear in him. Sure, he faced some serious adversity and the possibility of losing thousands of dollars in product. But he decided to respond rather than react like the people at the home office were doing. He said, "Son, just you watch. We've fallen into the crapper, but we're going to come out smelling like a rose."

My dad got on the phone for about forty-five minutes and called many of his best customers. He told them he had great news. He said his company had come across a significant shipment of quality strawberries in excellent quantity. Due to the overstock, the company had decided to offer them at a greatly reduced price, which would make a great deal for the client and preserve profits for the business. He told these customers he was offering the deal on a first come, first served basis to select clients first. It was theirs for the taking. But once they were gone, they were gone. Within what seemed like a matter of minutes, the strawberries were sold and my dad put down the phone. He smiled as he explained what had just happened, and we were off to have some real fun for the day.

I still catch myself applying this lesson. In business, obstacles always arise. I often find myself thinking, "How can I come out smelling like a rose?" Adversity truly is the best university. It introduces us to our other selves. Adversity forces us to find a way, and if we can't find one, we make one. We all pass through adversity.

The road to success is always under construction. Successful people know this and use adversity to their advantage.

ADVERSITY CAN BE A BIG STEPPING STONE

"Every failure brings with it the seed of an equivalent success."
— Napoleon Hill

I'd like to take the above statement a step further. I've found every failure, seeming downfall, disappointment, problem or challenge carries with it the seed of an equivalent or greater benefit. Depending on the mindset you choose to embrace, you will find that success or you won't. I know this principle is accurate because I've experienced it time and again. Most people, especially my dental patients, don't even know one of my biggest obstacles. Let me explain.

At the start of my third year of dental school, we student dentists were introduced to the dental clinic that served Omaha, Nebraska. We jumped into the clinic environment and began to see patients on a daily basis. That's when I learned I would face some adversity I could not have foreseen. The powdered latex gloves soon produced major skin irritations in my hands. I thought perhaps it would go away, but it didn't. It only became worse.

I met with the clinic director. He tried to reassure me and said with all his years in dentistry, he'd seen it all. I know he meant well, but in my case, he had no idea what he was talking about. He said he would switch me to powder-free latex gloves. He also told me to get some over-the-counter ointment that would surely knock out the red itchy rash on my hands. I switched to the powder-free gloves and did experience some relief for a few months. I still had the itchy rash, but it seemed to subside somewhat.

A few months later, the problems become worse. It was starting to get scary. I had reached the point of no return in dental school. I had already spent more than six years of my life at the University and many thousands of dollars to get to where I was. I had to figure out a solution. I went to a dermatologist, who said I appeared to be developing a latex allergy and recommended I use non-latex Nitrile gloves. He prescribed what he described as the strongest steroid ointment available at the highest concentration available. He also warned me to use it sparingly because through repeated use, my body would build up tolerance to it so it would lose its effectiveness over time.

On to the Nitrile gloves. Those gloves got me through dental school. I still had some issues, but things seemed to be under control. Graduation came and I left Nebraska and went to Idaho to start the practice of my dreams—from scratch. I worked hard to get things going for the first several months. Then it happened again! The blasted itchy rash came back and wouldn't go away. In fact, it got worse. I contacted glove manufacturers to find out what would be the best glove for me. I tried just about everything. I even tried using gauze liners under the gloves. Nothing worked.

Time to see another dermatologist. One dermatologist told me I needed to have patch testing to see what I was allergic to. She was not comfortable with my situation, so I went to another dermatologist in town. She saw my condition and agreed I needed to be patch tested if we were to have any chance of figuring out how to treat the problem. In the meantime, she gave me a cream that was sure to make things better if I used it eight-plus times per day. It did help, but sure made it hard to put my gloves on to do any dental work.

I fought through the persistent itchy rash for a few more years. Most dentists see patients at least four days a week. By the time I'd made it through three full days, my hands were beat up, battered, itchy and sometimes bleeding. The fourth day was brutal. I'd often wake in the middle of the night because the itching was so bad. The weekends were devoted to nursing my hands with lotions, the strongest steroid ointments on the market and the works—all to gear up for the next week. I saw a dermatopathologist in Utah who reminded me of the severity of the issue when he told me my livelihood was at stake. I already knew that, and it certainly didn't make me feel any better to hear it from him.

Finally, I gave in to the patch testing. I had to leave my business for five days and head to Utah to see a dermatology specialist, an expert for health care workers with glove issues. I'd been told that if anyone could shed some light on my situation, then he was the man. He took about 140 patches with different chemicals and taped them to my back. I wasn't permitted to shower for five days. Five itchy days later, I eagerly returned to the doctor to find out, once and for all, what I was allergic to. I wanted to know so I could avoid it and move forward.

Dr. Powell took all the patches off and was perplexed. He determined I was allergic to, drum roll please, NOTHING! The guru of dermatologists had no answers either! He recommended another lotion that was supposed to be better than all the rest and told me to call if I saw any improvement. The darned stuff just made my hands greasy and it was hard to get off.

Let's pause for a moment here. How would you have felt if you had a spouse, children, a mortgage, dental practice loans, minivan payments, thousands of dollars of debt from dental school, and had to struggle just to get through a week of work? All this and let's not forget the typical stresses that come with running a business and trying to turn a profit.

I reflected often on Napoleon Hill's statement about adversity and problems carrying with them the seed of an equivalent or greater success. I filled my mind with uplifting, positive and motivational material. I was determined to find a way to become successful, not in spite of the problem, but precisely *because* of it! Even some close dentist friends felt sorry for me. One of them said, "Oh Taylor, I'm sorry you have to go through this. I feel so bad for you."

All I could think was, "Yeah. Go ahead and feel sorry for me...all the way to the bank! This is going to be a huge stepping stone for me." I didn't know how it was going to happen, but I knew I was going to find a way to make this adversity slingshot me to success beyond anything I would have seen without it.

THE BIG BREAKTHROUGH

I learned an important lesson from T. Harv Eker: "Focus on obstacles and that's what you'll find. Focus on opportunities and that's what you'll find. What we focus on, expands."

How true that is! I focused on opportunities like never before. Incredible happenings soon began to unfold. First, I defied conventional wisdom by bringing on a full-time associate dentist. Then, I cut back to sixteen hours a week of dentistry and decided to work ON the business rather than being hands-on IN it all the time.

In early 2006, I came across an idea to run a dental assisting school in my office on Saturdays. I planned to train people to become dental assistants over a three-month period. They would participate in my accelerated course, which would include an emphasis on clinical hands-on learning. Students would be required to complete intense study at home during the week. The students would benefit because they wouldn't have to quit their jobs and would save $6,000-$9,000 in the process.

I took my plan to the Idaho State Boards of Dentistry and Education. I went back and forth with them for several months and finally my curriculum was approved—I had the green light to run the program. The first class was a huge success and I was off to the races! It was a winning program for the students, the dentists in the community and me. It's a rewarding business that provides great value to others and compensates me well. The best part is, I hired my excellent dental assistants and an associate doctor to run it mostly without my involvement. This leaves me with time to continue working ON the businesses in addition to being IN them.

Before long, I received a phone call from some doctors across the state. They wanted to run a dental assisting school in their office and had called the State Board of Dentistry. Can you guess what happened? The Board referred them to me! I saw an opportunity unfolding. I told the doctors they could figure it out themselves like I'd done, or I would license them to use my program. Further, I would help them start a school for an ongoing licensing fee for my services. They jumped right on that idea! I hired an attorney to draft a licensing agreement for these and other doctors to use my program. To make a long story short, they were a huge success from the beginning, even making headlines on the evening television news and in the newspapers.

I thought, "If I can do this once, then I can do it again, and again and again." In fact, I crunched some numbers to look at where I wanted to be financially by my thirty-eighth birthday. I decided to shoot for seventy-eight Assist To Succeed schools throughout the U.S. I quickly became too busy to do all the work myself. I called my first and best client and we became partners in the nationwide expansion of the dental assisting business. Now twenty-four dental offices in fifteen states are licensed to run the Assist To Succeed program. As I write this book, an additional five dentists have initiated the process to run Assist To Succeed schools in their offices. I've even had inquiries from dentists in Australia and the UK. My business has been featured multiple times on the NBC-TV affiliate in Boise. It has been featured on TV, radio and in newspapers across the United States.

Sometimes I wake up in the middle of the night now because I'm so excited about all the cool stuff going on. I get flashes of inspiration day and night that give my life juice. Oh, and now when I go to the mailbox, I get recurring checks to compensate me over and over again for my initial efforts! The skin problem? Though not gone, it's completely under control.

Was it easy to step outside the box and start these businesses? No. It was intimidating and sometimes downright scary. It was definitely the road less traveled by dentists—with no guarantee of success. But I had a secret weapon that helped me persist through it all. When doubt and fear reared its ugly head, all I had to do was look down at my beat-up itchy hands. That gave me the determination to find a way or make a way to succeed. My business success opened the doors to other business ventures that have proved quite profitable as well. Best part is, I feel like the fun has just begun and I'm just getting started. I wonder where I'd be right now if I hadn't faced adversity with my hands.

NO LEGS? NO PROBLEM.

I want to share a story about one of my dental patients, Amy Purdy. This remarkable woman lives in California, but recently visited her parents in Boise. Her parents recommended she come to me for some dental work. She was very pleasant, just like her parents.

I didn't think much about it until her mother stopped by the office not too long ago to give me a magazine. It was the January/February 2009 issue of *Muscle and Fitness: Hers* magazine. Inside was an impressive six-page article about how Amy had beaten the odds in overcoming severe adversity. It included fifteen color photos of Amy in different activities, including wakeboarding and snowboarding.

Amy's mother, Sherry, shared Amy's remarkable story with me. At age fourteen, Amy fell in love with snowboarding and became very good at it. Her dream was to travel the world and take her snowboard with her. Then the dark clouds of adversity covered the blue sky of her dreams when what seemed to be the flu turned into severe bacterial meningitis. Her hands and feet became purple, and she was quickly hospitalized and fell into a coma that lasted three weeks. Her doctors gave her a less than two percent chance of survival.

Amy remembers her thoughts during those dark moments. "I wasn't ready to give up. I didn't care if I lost my hands or feet. That's not what life's about." Fortunately, she regained use of her hands, but surgeons had to remove her feet. She lost her spleen and both kidneys were damaged. She lost nearly fifty pounds and most of her strength. A few years later, Amy received a life-saving gift from her father, who donated one of his kidneys.

"If you choose not to overcome adversity, then that's when you truly become disabled," Amy said.

Amy decided she'd never give in, despite the trauma that had nearly taken her life. Her dream of becoming an expert snowboarder was still alive, and she was determined to keep going until she reached it. And so, after seven grueling months of rehab, and with the ongoing support of her family, Amy was back on her snowboard. It wasn't smooth sailing at first, as her initial prosthetic lower legs didn't fit well and didn't allow many of the movements necessary to cut and maneuver like she wanted.

She was determined to find a way to get better prosthetics so she could perform the way envisioned. It was anything but easy.

Finally, after an exhaustive search, Amy found a leading prosthetics design and manufacturing company. The company developed cutting-edge prosthetics for both legs *and* decided to become Amy's sponsor. Soon she was back to competing again, and has since won several medals. She said, "I was so excited to be able to do it again." Amy says she has reached a point where she feels she is snowboarding even better than when she had legs!

As Amy reflects back on her hospital and recovery days, she wonders whether the process might have been easier had she been able to look to disabled role models in sports and the media, such as ESPN. She is passionate about helping other adaptive athletes find—and sustain—the courage to go after their dreams despite their adversities. She says, "You limit yourself so much when you don't know what's possible."

Today, Amy is a motivational speaker who seeks to inspire everyone, adaptive athletes in particular. By overcoming her own adversity, other doors have opened for Amy. In addition to motivational speaking, she has starred in a movie, modeled, serves as an advocate for Adaptive Action Sports, and has worked as a makeup artist. Amy has told me of her passion to inspire others to overcome their challenges and become the best they can be.

AN EXAM LIKE NO OTHER

Sometimes adversity comes in intense bursts without warning. When this happens, it's your job to keep your head up and retain unwavering focus. I'll conclude this chapter with the story of my clinical dental board exam, an example of what can happen when you remain focused during adversity.

As I've said before, I went to the university for eight years after high school and took hundreds of exams in preparation to become a dentist. If you combined all the exams I took during those eight years, none was as significant or challenging as the "final exam"—the last step—before I could become a dentist. The dental clinical board exam is a grueling three-day process. During this time dental school graduates, carefully scrutinized by examiners, perform clinical procedures on real patients. Everything I'd learned during my formal education culminated in this one final exam—my very future rested on its results.

I had put in tremendous effort to get to this point and prepare for this pivotal exam. I had lined up patients who needed the work I'd be tested on. I had even gone so far as to arrange back-up patients in case my "first string" patients couldn't be there up on test day. I was ready— or so I thought. Because once the three-day exam began, I encountered some challenges I couldn't have ever anticipated or prepared for.

My wife Jannie and I were expecting our third child—and her delivery date was three weeks away. We already had a four-year-old son and a two-year-old daughter. Well, I faced an unplanned challenge with all four of them (including our unborn baby) right in the middle of the three-day test.

The first day went well. I did a good job and everything went according to plans.

The second day of the exam was stressful. I was on pins and needles, worried my wife could go into labor at any time. I didn't have a cell phone, so I had to rely on the administrative staff to alert me in the event of an emergency phone call.

My anxiety was heightened because it was time for the dreaded "root canal" section of the exam. We had a limited time to complete the procedure on a laboratory tooth. Every step had to be done well in a quick and concise manner. I began, but right in the middle of the procedure, I was paged from the third floor lab to the second floor to take an "important" phone call. All I could think was, "My wife!" I was worried she'd gone into labor and needed me.

I checked out of the exam and bolted for the second floor to take the call while precious exam time ticked away. I was out of breath when I arrived to take the call. I managed to say hello and, to my utter dismay, found I had been paged to take a non-urgent call from a patient. Someone should have taken a message! I was furious as I dashed back to the third floor to try to make up for lost time with my root canal.

I had lost about seven minutes and realized I wouldn't have enough time to complete all the steps needed. With a root canal, you check your accuracy by taking x-rays. I didn't have time for x-rays. I did my best and finished, having no idea how I'd done. To avoid a harsh penalty for going over the allocated time, I handed in my work—such as it was. I gathered my things and headed for home thinking, "Did I just blow my chances to pass the most important exam of my life?"

All the way home I thought, "If I can just hang on and make the last day of the exam my very best day, then I still have a chance to pass this. I *know* I can make up for the points I lost today."

But when I got home that day, the *real* troubles began.

During dinner, Jannie said she'd been having more contractions and thought it was time to call the doctor. She told me our two-year-old daughter, Taylie, had a cold and it was getting worse. She also told me our four-year-old son Ty had been playing with his little buddy from next door. They'd been "sword-fighting" with sticks and somehow Ty had been poked in the eye. The white part of his right eye was turning red and a steady stream of tears dripped from that eye. That, combined with the swelling, did not look good.

We needed to make two urgent phone calls. First, we called the doctor about Ty's eye. They said it sounded like an emergency and told us to take him to the emergency room at once.

On to phone call number two. Jannie called *her* doctor about her contractions and symptoms. They said she was probably in labor and that we should get her to the hospital right away.

With the combined stress of these urgent family situations and the intense pressure of the board exam, all I could do was take a few deep breaths and keep going. I made arrangements for someone to stay with Taylie so I could take Ty and Jannie to the hospital. I took her upstairs, got her in her pajamas, and brushed her teeth. With everything else going on, I hadn't paid much attention to Taylie's bad cold. But when I opened her mouth to brush her back teeth, I was stunned by what I saw! She had a highly inflamed throat with purulent exudates. That's just a fancy way of saying her throat was bright red and covered with pus. I'd learned about strep throat and was sure I was staring directly at a severe case of it.

What to do? We called the doctor's office and described Taylie's symptoms. They said her situation was urgent, and advised us to take her to the emergency room, too! Thoughts such as, "Why is this happening? Why all at once? Why now? What am I supposed to do?" raced through my mind.

What would you have done if you'd been in my shoes?

When you find yourself in a crisis, it's important for you to take decisive, consistent, positive action towards your desired results.

I did the only thing I could do. I kept moving. I kept at it. I put one foot in front of the other and fought off any thoughts of giving up. My family means the world to me and I wasn't about to let them down. Not then; not now; not ever!

I drew the line and told the hospital I could only manage to take my wife and son in at the same time. I told them I'd take my daughter in the next day. After all, Taylie's breathing was fine and she was able to swallow. I left her with the babysitter and took Jannie and Ty to the hospital.

We rushed to the hospital and when we got there, I took Jannie to the labor and delivery unit first. They started an IV and got her hooked up to the fancy medical equipment. Once I saw she was "situated," I took Ty and headed for the emergency room, which happened to be all the way at the other end of the huge hospital!

After examining Ty, the attending physician expressed her concern for his situation. She was worried about the bacterial infection that was out of control. She placed dye in his eye and studied his eye under ultraviolet light. After what seemed an eternity, she medicated his eye with ointment, gave me care instructions and sent us on our way. By this time, it was one o'clock in the morning. Finally, I could join my wife in labor and delivery.

When I got to her room, I got caught up on the situation. Jannie was still having frequent contractions but seemed stable. I sat on the couch while my exhausted boy drifted into quiet slumber. My thoughts went to the stressful exam I'd completed hours ago. Day three, the final day, was to begin at 6:30 a.m., just five short hours away.

Not even an hour had passed before a completely new problem developed. The attending physician told us he was concerned because the baby's heart rate had become abnormal. He seemed perplexed until he came to the conclusion that the baby had a nuchal cord. This condition occurs when the umbilical cord gets wrapped around the baby's head and the pressure can cut off the oxygen supply. Though labor wasn't progressing, the doctor told me he wanted to keep Jannie there for the night for close monitoring.

What was I to do? Bless Jannie's heart. She said I should take Ty home and try to take a nap before the last day of my exam. I headed for home, put Ty to bed, set several alarm clocks, and climbed into bed, exhausted. About 90 minutes later, I woke up and quickly prepared to head to the dental clinic to finish the darn test. I called the hospital to see how Jannie was doing. She said the nuchal chord stuff had gone away and they were sending her home, calling it "false labor".

So at six o'clock in the morning, I called my neighbor and asked if he would go to the hospital and bring home my precious wife while his wife watched our kids. Finally, things seemed to be under control, and I could focus on getting through what remained of the nightmare of an exam. I made it to the dental school on time and began the exam.

For the final portion of the exam, our assignment was to remove severe tarter build-up from the teeth of an individual who hadn't had a professional dental cleaning in a long time. Thankfully, my patient showed up and I went to work. To my dismay, it proved to be an extremely difficult case. The tarter was tenacious and felt like concrete. Given the situation, I did the only thing I could do. I kept at it. I kept moving forward. I did what I could, and I did the best I could do.

Midway through the exam, my patient grew bored and wanted to call it quits for the day. Obviously, this guy had no idea how much pressure I was under and how important it was for me to finish his cleaning. He had no concept of the consequences I'd face if he left. But he'd made a commitment to let me clean his teeth for my exam and I wasn't about to let him break that commitment. Then he said he needed to use the restroom. I told my student assistant to follow him, and added, "No matter what, DO NOT let him out of this building!" Fortunately, the guy came back. I finished up and sent him to be evaluated by the examiners.

It was noon and I had finished the beast of an exam. At that point, I didn't care about anything other than getting out of there and rushing home to see my wife. When I opened the front door, I couldn't believe what I saw! There was Jannie, on the floor, red faced and sweating in intense pain. She managed some words between contractions: "It's time. Let's go!" With my heart pounding and adrenaline racing once again, I put her in the car. I quickly recruited a babysitter and we left for the hospital again.

Although we rushed to the hospital, we barely got there in time. There was no time for an epidural, let alone time for the doctor to get there. Forty-five minutes after I'd walked in the door after finishing my dental board exam, our third child was crying for the first time. He was a beautiful baby and the delivery had gone well. Finally, I was able to sit down, take a deep breath and collect my thoughts. After I saw Jannie was cared for, and after holding my new son for a few minutes, my focus turned to Taylie and getting her throat evaluated and treated.

I went and got my daughter and took her to the hospital emergency room. The ER doctor confirmed what I'd suspected—strep throat—and started her on antibiotics. She warned me to keep Taylie away from her mom and the new baby because she was still highly contagious. I didn't care and neither did Jannie. Enough was enough. I needed to see how Jannie and the baby were and let the kids know everything was going to be okay.

Moments later, I glanced outside and noticed the afternoon sky had suddenly become very dark. Then a voice on the hospital PA system announced a tornado warning had been issued for the entire county. I wasn't about to be stranded in the hospital with two sick kids to create a risk—not to mention a big inconvenience—for my new baby and exhausted wife. I kissed Jannie goodbye, then grabbed Ty and Taylie and headed for the car.

We headed home, but hadn't gotten halfway there before the dark Omaha sky opened and dropped a severe hailstorm on us, complete with winds and some of the biggest hail I'd ever seen. The large hailstones began to pelt the car. The kids were frightened (maybe I was a little frightened, too!) so I stopped under an overpass until the storm subsided. The moment came and I made a break for home.

We arrived home safely, although I can't say the same for the car. The day and the big exam were finally over. *At last!* I fed the kids and put them to bed. All I could do was sit in wonder and amazement and think about everything that had happened during those three days. I felt battered and worn out. But I was still breathing. I figure as long as I'm breathing, I still have a chance. I'd done my very best and I hadn't given up. Now all I could do was wait.

Though I'd done my best on the dental exam, I was still worried about the results I'd receive in the next six weeks. Failing the exam means you have to wait months to retake it. You have to pay the fees all over again, line up more patients, and fly them and yourself to another state and go through "board exam stress" one more time. I certainly didn't want to do that!

The big day finally came. I saw the white envelope containing my board exam results. That envelope contained my very future—the proclamation of whether I could practice dentistry or not. With my heart pounding, I sat down, took a deep breath and opened the envelope. *I passed!* By just doing my best, I'd handled family and professional challenges all through the exam, welcomed a new son—and made it through what had been the most difficult experience of my life to that point.

There were times during that three-day exam when I could have easily given up, but didn't. I learned that despite the toughest circumstances, we *can* overcome adversity. I learned that despite the outlook, if we'll try the "up look" and stay focused on doing our best, then we can succeed in spite of, and in many cases *because* of adversity. To this day, the hail dents in my car serve as a powerful reminder to me that tough times don't last, but tough people do!

Summary

I have thoroughly enjoyed writing this chapter. Overcoming adversity and becoming the better because of it is never easy. However, it is always rewarding and always worth the effort. Truly, adversity is the best university. Remember, the refiner's fire produces the purest of gold. Coal put under intense prolonged pressure can yield a diamond. Impure or contaminated clear water can be placed over a fire and boiled, and within minutes, it becomes purified. Just as the heat of the fire brings the water to a boil and kills the impurities, your own fire to conquer adversity can free you from the impurities of failure that would otherwise hold you back.

Perhaps you're facing some adversity right now. Whether you are going through adversity now or face it in the future, I challenge you to search for the equivalent or greater success that can result from it. I assure you, success is always there for the optimistic seeker of opportunities. It's there for the individual who does not recognize failure as a final result. You will truly learn some of life's most valuable lessons from the university of adversity.

CHAPTER 13

Get There Faster With a Coach

*"The dream begins with a teacher who believes in you,
who tugs and pushes and leads you to the next plateau,
sometimes poking you with a sharp stick called truth."*
— Dan Rather

Over the years, I've met some really neat people with fascinating stories. I remember having lunch in the dental school cafeteria with some fellow students. One of them, I'll call him Don, shared a story from when he was home before dental school started. He and some buddies were at a park playing pick-up basketball. I can just imagine the scene. A bunch of college guys trying to relive their high school glory days through a game of basketball.

One day, Don and the guys were playing when a nice car pulled up to the park. A tall athletic-looking African American man stepped out and approached them. As he got closer, they realized it was Michael Jordan!

He asked, "Do you mind if I play?" Can you imagine having the best player in the history of the game just show up at a park and ask to play ball with you? They were ecstatic! This took place during the years after Michael Jordan's first retirement. He later went on to lead the

Chicago Bulls to three more NBA championships to add to his previous three.

Don's assignment was to guard Michael Jordan. I still laugh when I remember his description of the experience. Don got into his best defensive stance and made an all-out effort to defend the great one. He watched the ball go up and down as Jordan dribbled. He closely monitored the ball and tried to time the exact moment to lunge in for the steal. Once it came, he lunged hard. All he caught was air and immediately saw Jordan in a completely different position with a "What in the world are you thinking, kid?" look on his face. Then Jordan said, "You reach, I teach." And in a flash, he blew by Don for a dunk.

Several years after Don told us that story, I heard motivational speaker James Malinchak at a conference. He told of a time when he had shared the speaking platform with Michael Jordan. He passed on some thoughts Jordan shared that day. Jordan acknowledged that many people regarded him as a great basketball player, maybe even the best ever. However, Jordan went on to explain that no matter how good he was, he had always needed a coach. Phil Jackson brought out the best in him. He picked up on things as the game unfolded that Jordan sometimes didn't see. That guidance, along with incredible athletic ability, hard work and determination, made Jordan virtually unstoppable for years.

EVERYBODY NEEDS A COACH

Several times throughout this book, I've shared my positive experiences with coaches and mentors. What is a coach? It's someone who is skilled and expert and can help you get where you want to go.

When it comes to mentors, I've probably mentioned Zig Ziglar more than anyone. He has been my mentor for years—especially during the years I've experienced significant personal growth and business success. One of the greatest lessons I've learned from him is to attend what he refers to as "Automobile University." He claims we can learn far more by taking advantage of pockets of dead time than we may ever realize.

For example, what do you listen to when you're driving or taking mass transit to work? Chances are, you probably listen to the radio. I'd venture to say you probably already know about the power of continuous learning. Maybe you already benefit from "Automobile University." The idea is to identify any dead time during your day and use that time to fill your mind with positive and educational information. I've purchased many of Ziglar's audio training materials, and over the years, I know I've listened to his main motivational programs probably more than fifteen times each. It's important to keep listening because as Ziglar says, "Repetition is the mother of all learning. That makes it the father of action and the architect of accomplishment."

Why not take advantage of your down time? I'm amazed to think about how much I've learned in the years since I finished my "formal" education. Sure, I gained a tremendous amount of knowledge at the University. However, the majority of my learning has taken place after my classroom education was complete. I'll share one of Zig Ziglar's philosophies on lifelong learning: "When I'm sitting, I'm reading. When I'm moving, I'm listening." People ask me all the time, "How on earth do you find the time to read all those books and listen to all those audio recordings?" I have one answer, "Automobile University."

Mentors and coaches come in many forms. A mentor could be someone you associate with regularly. You could find mentoring in the form of books, audio programs, DVDs, webinars and teleconferences, among other things. Mentors can be parents, siblings, friends, business associates, or people you run into from time to time. It doesn't matter what form your coaches take. What's important is to have coaches in one form or another in life and during your career.

Brian Tracy has been another important coach. I've gained from his knowledge and expertise through the written word, Internet videos, audio programs and E-books—mostly through iLearningGlobal (I'll talk about this in a future chapter) and teleconference calls. Brian believes everyone should seek out mentors and coaches. He says, "You can never learn it all on your own. You'll never live that long."

Brian uses an analogy to illustrate the power of coaches and mentors. Are you familiar with Germany's Autobahn? It's a super freeway with no speed limits so you can reach your destination quickly. Then there are rocky mountain dirt roads that wind around and it takes forever to get where you're going. Tracy says having proper coaches and mentors is the surest way to put you on—and keep you on—the Autobahn of life. Having good coaches and mentors empowers you to feel comfortable enough to push the gas pedal down and get where you're going faster.

My dad remains the most important coach in my life. He has been a fountain of wisdom and pillar of strength for me. I'm fortunate that I can draw on his expert advice and counsel for almost anything. He's one of the most successful and well-rounded people I know. His ongoing mentoring has served as the foundation of all the major progress I've made. I know everyone hasn't been blessed with great parents like I have. My mother is right up there with my dad in providing me the encouragement, wisdom and insight I so highly treasure. Together they make a great team.

You'll find coaches and mentors are a key to your success. While your parents might not serve as your role models, the coaches and mentors you need are out there. No matter what your circumstances, you can find coaches and mentors to help you get there faster than you could by yourself. Get a coach and get there faster!

BUILDING A BUSINESS

When I started my dental practice more than six years ago, I learned some tough lessons right away. I learned it was going to take more than putting my name and credentials on the door to bring people in for services. And so, I made what turned out to be a great decision. With some trepidation (after all, I *was* a very new business owner), I spent six thousand dollars and hired a coach to help me develop a plan to get my business off to a fast start. Then I flew to Phoenix for three days of training, and had six months of follow-up support afterward. That decision proved to be the key to getting my business on the road to success.

A few years later, I hired a coach in Chicago and joined his dentist coaching club. He's two years younger than I am, but that didn't matter to me. I knew right away that he was a brilliant marketer and businessman. I learned as much as I could from him for a few years and my dental practice saw significant growth as a result. I have different coaches today, but I still use many of the success principles I learned from him.

Mentors and coaches are everywhere. Do your research. Ask questions. Seek and you will find. Some coaches cost a lot of money and some cost nothing at all. Don't overlook a coach because of the fees involved. Remember, it's all about your return on investment. Would you give one hundred dollars if you could learn how to get one thousand dollars back? I'll play that game all day long! Your investment in hiring a coach may be some of the best money you'll ever spend.

THE THREE RULES OF LIFE

Almost twenty years ago, my dad attended a seminar where the legendary coach Lou Holtz was speaking. That day, Holtz, former coach of the Notre Dame Fighting Irish, shared his family philosophy. It's one he has also shared with his football players. He called this philosophy "The Three Rules of Life." After the seminar, my dad came home and wrote those rules on the back of his business cards and gave one to each of us kids. He taught us what Holtz taught him.

Recently, I wrote a letter to Coach Lou Holtz to thank him for the impact his three rules have had on my life. Here's an excerpt from that January 2009 letter:

Dear Mr. Holtz,

My name is Dr. Taylor Clark and I'm from Boise, Idaho. I am a dentist, dental business consultant, coach and motivational speaker. I am writing a motivational book about success in life and business through beating any odds we might face.

When I was a teenager, my father attended a seminar where you were a speaker. When he came home, he told me about your three rules of life, then wrote them on the back of his business card and gave me the card.

1. Do your best.

2. Do what is right.

3. Treat others the way you would like them to treat you.

That battered, beat-up business card meant a lot to me and your rules are a part of me today. Thank you so much!

I would like to share your rules in my book and would love to have a moment of your time to discuss them with you. It would be a great honor for me. You can reach me on my personal cell.

Kind Regards,

Taylor Clark, DDS

Shortly after I sent the letter, I was pleasantly surprised to receive a phone call from Coach Holtz. I thanked him for everything he'd done to motivate and inspire me. Then I asked whether he would talk a little more about his philosophy. Here are a few thoughts he shared with me:

"We've had these core values in our family over the past forty years. I've never known anybody who didn't succeed by using these three rules. People complicate life too much. If you'll just follow these rules, things will work out."

At one point during our conversation, I was writing fast and furiously. There was a pause and Coach Holtz said, "Are you still there?"

I replied, "Yes! I'm just writing as fast as I can." So he continued. He said something that immediately helped me become a better father. After all, being a great father and husband is right at the top of my list.

He said, "When your children most need love and understanding is usually when they deserve it the least." I've thought about that many times—it's changed how I react when my children misbehave. Loving them unconditionally, even when they misbehave, has already had a positive impact in our home.

SUMMARY

Think of all the wisdom floating around out there! Life can be much easier and meaningful if you follow the lead of someone you admire and respect. You can avoid mistakes when you learn from the experiences of others. You can beat the odds much faster with the help of the experts.

Be coached, and when the time is right, be ready to coach somebody else. The tables will turn one day, if they haven't already. You'll become so good at some things that you'll be able to coach others to success. It's important to remember where you came from. When you do, you'll embrace the opportunity to lift others up and help them get what they want. Do that, and your own life will be enriched and more meaningful.

And now for one last thought. The people I revere as most successful in any endeavor know there will never come a day when they no longer need to be coached. The best performers in any field always have a coach or mentor, no matter what their level of success.

No matter how high you go, you can *always* learn more and climb higher. Having a coach and listening to that coach will help you to avoid what T. Harv Eker calls the three most dangerous words a person can say: "I know that." Successful people constantly learn and grow. Unsuccessful people think they already know.

CHAPTER 14

Face Your Fears

"Let me assert my firm belief that the only thing we have to fear is fear itself."
— Franklin D. Roosevelt

If you asked me to name the #1 reason people don't reach their full potential, my answer would be **fear**. Fear is a roadblock that stymies progress and keeps many people from even getting started.

Let's take a moment to explore the components of fear. I've come across what I believe to be the best way to understand fear. FEAR is an acronym for <u>F</u>alse <u>E</u>vidence <u>A</u>ppearing <u>R</u>eal. Many times, we allow our fears to keep us from making progress toward achieving our goals.

Have you ever been so afraid of something that just thinking about it made your heart pound and gave you sweaty palms? It's certainly happened to me!

Shortly after high school, I obtained my commercial driver's license and began to deliver produce using the large white box trucks. I remember well the summer of 1992 because I turned nineteen that summer. One day, my assignment was to take the last load of the day: several thousand dollars' worth of high quality produce—raspberries, strawberries and blueberries, among other things. I was taking it to a store that required its orders to be on pallets and sealed with shrink-wrap, to make one unit.

Something happened with the delivery to give me a heavy dose of fear. The veteran workers at the warehouse helped me put the entire order on a pallet and we loaded it into the truck. It was a tall pallet and they placed it up in the corner. I didn't have experience driving a load like that. I didn't know much about the use of load locks to secure the loads, either. Looking back, I have a hunch those guys knew I might be in for it. I closed the truck's overhead door, pulled out of the warehouse and was off to the delivery. I had never been to that particular store, but I had directions to get there. It was crazy! The trip involved crazy bumps in the road, railroad tracks and many turns. I didn't know, but if you hit a bump in the road and it made the truck rock, it's a truck driver's nightmare. No matter, I discovered it soon enough.

Finally, I found the store and backed up to the loading dock. As I rolled up the truck's door, to my dismay, I saw lots of blueberries rolling around. I quickly surveyed the scene and saw other berries and produce scattered all over the floor. My heart sank and I couldn't believe what I saw. The entire load had dumped. I'd never seen such a produce mess. Before I had time to react, the store foreman came over and looked in utter disgust at the mess. He grunted under his breath and said, "Send it all back!" Then he walked away and I was left to face the huge mess. I felt two inches tall.

When I got back to the warehouse, our foreman was still there. He opened the truck and gathered the damaged produce. Much of it had to be discarded. I was devastated! I felt horrible because the company had lost money and it was my fault.

Then the foreman said the load should have been better secured and told me he'd "been there; done that." I'll tell you what, after that experience I had no confidence in my ability to deliver produce. I wanted to quit. I was overcome by fear, just thinking I might have to make another large delivery.

Finally, I decided to respond to the experience rather than react to it. I decided I wasn't going to let it get the best of me. I learned a valuable lesson from dumping that load; one I'll never forget: **Face your fear and the fear disappears!**

Over the next few work summers, I took any load I could get. It wasn't long before I took loads double and quadruple the size of the load I'd dumped. I'll admit that at first, I got that familiar feeling in the pit of my stomach every time I backed into a dock. Then slowly, I opened the overhead door just to make sure no oranges or anything else were rolling around on the floor. I learned how to pack the loads tightly and secure them with load locks. Before long, I gained tremendous confidence. I don't drive produce trucks these days, but I still benefit from the confidence I gained as a result of overcoming that fear.

What fears are holding you back? What big loads are ready for you to take? I challenge you to think about your fears and how they're holding you back. It's time to move forward and take decisive action to alleviate those fears and watch as magic unfolds before your eyes. As you face your fears, those fears will disappear.

COURAGE IS ACTING IN SPITE OF FEAR

No one will forget that dreadful day. September 11, 2001. Terrorists attacked the city of New York in the biggest and worst terrorist attack ever on U.S. soil. What many of us may not know is Mayor Rudolph Giuliani was stuck in a building near Ground Zero when the first tower fell. Imagine how you might have felt as you stared at the TV, helpless, as one of the Twin Towers crashed down, knowing you and thousands of others might die. Even worse, how would you have felt knowing all eyes were on you to lead the City through this unprecedented disaster?

Years earlier, Giuliani prepared for such a moment, largely through lessons he'd learned from his father. Shortly before his father's death, Giuliani asked his dad whether he'd ever been afraid of anything. His father told him courage isn't the absence of fear, but rather the management of fear. And in those dark days after September 11, Giuliani heard his father's words many times: "Courage is doing what you have to do even though you are afraid." Never one to bow down to obstacles, Giuliani said, "If you let fear, worry and doubt overcome you, you will lose the battle. Pessimistic leaders always fail."

Knowing the people around him trapped in that building, the people of New York City—and the entire United States—would look to him as a leader, his father's wisdom also helped Giuliani during the unprecedented chaos and fear of that day. Giuliani's father had once advised, "In a crisis, when everybody else gets very, very excited, you have to become the calmest person in the room, so you can figure a way out of the situation."

After the first tower came down, Giuliani knew his and the lives of thousands around him were in jeopardy. Although seemingly trapped in the building, they tried to escape through the basement, but the doors were locked. In that moment of intense emotion, Giuliani remembered the lessons learned from his father. He forced himself to become calm and regain his composure. He focused intensely on surviving and helping others survive. He had to act quickly and wisely to ignite hope in those who surrounded him. With this mindset, they were able to find a way out to safety.

We all saw what happened when the second tower fell. With no thought for their own safety, a host of firefighters, law enforcement officers, emergency workers and civilians worked to save more than twenty thousand lives that day. Giuliani said, "Thanks to the bravery of these men and women, the worst attack on American soil became the most successful rescue operation in American history. Never before have I witnessed such courage."

RETIRING NUMBER 16

Several years ago, I was privileged to fly to San Francisco to watch my brother Greg and the 49ers on Monday Night Football. The game was fun and I was proud to see Greg excel at such a high level. I was in for a surprise that night. At halftime, I watched as the 49ers honored the great quarterback Joe Montana and retired Montana's jersey number, #16. Having led the 49ers to four Super Bowl championships, Joe Montana is regarded by many as the greatest quarterback in NFL history.

What makes great people great? I read about Joe Montana and enjoyed what he said about greatness. Montana learned that in order to be great, you cannot be afraid to fail. He knew his performance was watched by millions of people, week in and week out. Instead of worrying about every little mistake, he just went out and did the best job he could. When he made a mistake, he knew those TV viewers saw it. Besides that, he was forced to relive his mistakes again in slow motion with critiques from his coaches. Confronting his mistakes taught him to overcome his fear of failure.

"I learned to fail fast, learn from my mistakes and move on. Why beat yourself up about it? Just do better next time." — Joe Montana

FACING A GIANT

Remember the Bible story of David and Goliath, where little David slays the mighty Goliath? The 2000 Sydney Olympics featured a modern-day version of David and Goliath. I remember watching the great event on TV as it happened. As a former wrestler, I was very interested in seeing the American underdog, Rulon Gardner, go up against the "Russian Bear," Alexander Karelin, who was considered the greatest Greco-Roman wrestler of all time. He had three gold medals, nine world titles and no losses in international competition during the thirteen years leading up to the final gold medal match against Gardner.

Karelin was huge and intimidating. I was scared on Gardner's behalf, just watching Karelin on TV! The commentators talked about what an underdog Gardner was. They said if Gardner beat Karelin, it would be the greatest upset in wrestling history.

At least one person in the millions of fans and viewers thought Gardner could win it—and that was Rulon Gardner himself. Instead of giving into fear of failure, Gardner courageously faced the "Goliath" of wrestling. He shocked Karelin by scoring one point during the first round. Never giving into fear, Gardner fought hard and wore the great Russian down. Time began to tick away and the impossible began to seem possible. As the last few seconds ticked off the clock, Gardner would not be denied as he shocked the world. The place erupted in cheers as the world witnessed, and the U.S. celebrated, the historic event.

Facing your fears gives you an opportunity to grow. You'll never know what greatness you're capable of unless you fill yourself with courage and conquer those tasks you've been afraid to try because of fear. Some of your greatest triumphs and accomplishments will come as a result of what happens as you overcome your deepest fears.

SUMMARY

I've learned something from many of my mentors and the experts over the years. Success principles exist and they are what they are. Those of us who are open to learn and follow them will be able to experience the sweet fruits these principles yield.

I've also learned a lesson about doubt and fear. No matter what it takes, you need to work to eliminate these negative emotions from your life. Doubt and fear have never accomplished anything and never will. If you expect to beat the odds in life, you'll have to overcome these two enemies that stand in your way.

> *"If you want the good fruit,*
> *you've got to go out on the limb and get it."*
> — Cliff Clark

Again, as my Grandpa Clark taught me, it's essential to take advantage of opportunities, take risks and move forward—facing our fears. The best way I know to combat fears is to face them regularly and often. Getting busy and taking action to solve fearful situations is the magic formula to make them disappear.

Opportunities abound for everyone. When you focus on your opportunities rather than your fear of failure, you'll give yourself a chance to win. Get ready as best as you can, as fast as you can and then get started even if you're not fully ready. Perfection is paralysis. You can't allow yourself to fall into the trap of paralysis by analysis. Sometimes you need to jump off that cliff of fear. Don't worry—you'll grow wings or find a parachute on the way down. Face your fears, and then those fears will disappear!

CHAPTER 15

Win Through Owning a Business

"An investment in knowledge pays the best interest."
— Benjamin Franklin

In 2007, I went to a seminar about creating wealth. It was attended by investors and business owners from around the world. I gained a lot of knowledge and discovered new ways to look at what I already knew. It was great to hear the experts talk about the principles of creating wealth.

Then, Sandy Botkin got up to speak. Botkin had been a top attorney for the IRS and trained new IRS attorneys. He left his government job and now helps business owners learn about the tremendous tax advantages available to them. He also helps people who don't own businesses understand why they need to become business owners as soon as possible.

Before I go any further, I need to remind you: I'm not an attorney or an accountant. I don't claim to be an expert in any of these areas and am not qualified to give tax or legal advice. However, I am an informed business entrepreneur who is passionate about learning and applying the principles of success and wealth. That being said, I'll continue with what I learned that day in 2007.

I enjoyed everything Botkin said. Some of it made me angry and some of it made me happy. I learned about tax laws and rules applicable to business. I'd been a business owner for several years, but missed out on saving a substantial amount of money because I didn't know about the many tax laws written to my advantage. I'd read quite a bit about the subject, and now it was starting to come together.

I learned tax-saving strategies I'd missed. That's when I started to get excited. I saw the light and saw how I could better accumulate wealth as I moved forward. It became clear that business ownership is a powerful wealth-building tool everyone should consider.

Don't get me wrong. I'm a happy, law-abiding citizen of this great country and regard it a privilege to pay my taxes. However, I sure don't want to pay any more than I'm legally obligated to pay. I know there's no one back in Washington to look out for my individual financial interests. It's my responsibility to keep up with the tax laws and determine how best to apply them to my situation. It's *my* responsibility to choose competent legal and financial advisors to help me make decisions to my advantage.

WEALTH 101

According to the IRS publication, "Personal Wealth," there was approximately $15 trillion in accumulated wealth in the U.S. in the early 1990's. According to a more recent study by Merrill Lynch, personal wealth in the U.S. has now climbed to more than $27 trillion. There's something interesting about this. Nearly ninety percent of this wealth is owned by only ten percent of the people.

Are you thinking what I'm thinking? What do the wealthy ten percent know that the other ninety percent don't? It's a simple, yet vital piece of knowledge. The wealthy ten percent understand the quickest way to accumulate wealth is through owning a business. I've been on both sides. For years, I was an employee with a job. Now, I've owned a business for several years. When it comes to accumulating wealth, I see big differences between the two.

WORKING HARD FOR YOUR MONEY

During my teenage and college years, I held jobs that paid by the hour. With the intense study that comes with being a full-time student, I had a hard time putting in many hours at work. But during the summer, I learned to "make hay while the sun shines." I learned about overtime and developed a love/hate relationship with it. Getting paid one and one-half times my hourly wage was great! Then something happened that really bothered me. Summer is the busy season in the produce business, so it was common to work more than seventy hours a week. When my paycheck arrived, the gross pay was high, but the net pay hadn't increased like I'd thought it would. Then the reality hit me hard: The more you make, the more they take!

Through learning about work, income and taxes, I found something else that bothered me. Years ago, in the typical family, the father went to work every day to bring home the bacon, while the mother stayed home to nurture the children. Today, it's common for both parents to have full-time jobs. In some instances, such as when the mother goes back to work after having a baby, the net effect on the family's income is not that great. By the time you figure in net income after taxes, childcare costs, transportation costs and other expenses, the result is not impressive. In some cases, the net increase in household income is almost zero.

Accumulating wealth often doesn't happen for those who earn a salary. This is important for anyone who wants to become wealthy. Approximately ninety-seven percent of Americans who are financially independent own a business. Owning a business opens the door for them to enjoy some huge tax advantages.

HAVING YOUR MONEY WORK HARD FOR YOU

Imagine for a moment you have a bucket of water. The bucket represents your financial life and the water represents the money you've earned. We all have a bucket and the buckets have one thing in common—all the buckets have holes in them. Some buckets have more holes than others, but everyone's bucket has at least some holes in it. It doesn't take a genius to realize that with more and bigger holes, you'll need to add more water to your bucket just to keep it from emptying out. The holes in your bucket can be varied and extensive. You may have living expenses, mortgage payments or rent, student loan bills, debt payments, taxes, medical bills, tuition, interest costs and on and on.

The biggest drains on our financial buckets are taxes and interest. These two financial "hole-pokers" steal a great deal from the typical household budget and represent the majority of holes in our buckets.

Do you know how much you spend each year on taxes alone? If you don't know, then I urge you to take time to calculate that amount so you'll know where to start in order to improve in the next year. A good CPA or certified financial advisor can help you minimize your tax burden. Do you know how much money you spent last year on interest in all forms (credit cards, mortgage, automobile loans, student loans, home equity loans, etc.)?

I recommend two actions to plug the holes in your bucket quickly and eliminate the biggest drains on your finances. First, stop borrowing money and start an aggressive debt repayment program. Get help if you need it. Second, start a home-based business so you can begin to reduce your tax burden right away.

At this point, you'll be meeting your living expenses and have some money set aside for future needs. Then you'll have more money available for wise investments. Families whose money is well managed don't pay interest—they earn it. With a steady amount of money now going to interest-bearing investments, you'll experience the exponential power of compounding interest—not the crushing effects of compounding taxes.

ELIMINATING DEBT

Are you in debt? Do you watch each month as chunks of money go out to repaying your debts? If so, then I have some encouraging news for you. You can become financially independent! But you must immediately focus on being *financially independent*. Do NOT focus on *debt* or *being in debt*.

Remember the Law of Attraction. What we focus on expands. Focusing on debt just brings us more debt. That's why it's essential to stay focused on financial independence, while faithfully sticking to an automatic debt repayment plan. Soon, your debts will disappear, one by one. It's vital to think only about abundance. The opportunities and means to prosper financially will come fast as you remain focused on abundance. When you've eliminated one debt, simply add that amount to the next debt. Now you have more money each month to send to the next creditor. Finally, you'll have a large amount of money going to pay off your last debt.

People who pay off debt have an advantage over those who don't. That's encouraging news. Let me explain. The magic begins when you've paid off the last of your debt. By the time it happens, you've developed the discipline to spend a substantial amount of money each month. You've already established the habit and you're used to not seeing that money. So what should you do after everything is paid off? You should keep paying it out! The difference is now you get to decide where your money will go. You get to build a financial reserve and plant those little money seeds out and watch as they start growing. It's much easier for you who have paid off your debts just to redirect that money to income producing areas than it is for someone, with or without debt, to try to start a new habit by dedicating money toward monthly investments. You get to use the discipline you developed to your advantage. This experience of paying off your debt can be very rewarding.

STARTING A HOME-BASED BUSINESS

We've already discussed the tremendous tax advantages for business owners. Now comes the fun part. What type of home-based business should you choose? I'm not going to go into the different ways to structure a business and the many home-based business opportunities available. If you want a broad and detailed description of all the options out there, then I recommend Robert Allen's book, *Multiple Streams of Income*. He provides great insight into the many businesses you can operate from home. In this chapter, I want to narrow the focus to the one option I believe gives people the best chance to succeed.

Referral, or network, marketing is a powerful and legitimate way to do business from home. Network marketing? Yes. I realize the words often carry a stigma. I'd like to change that.

In the past, some network marketing businesses and their representatives didn't do business ethically. I'm not talking here about filling your garage with lotions, potions, soaps and useless knick-knacks no one will ever need. I have no disrespect, of course, for any legitimate products as long as somebody derives benefits from them.

Let me tell you about the network marketing industry's smart and savvy methods for distributing products or services. Having studied business and been in business for years, I've learned about the billions of dollars businesses spend to promote their products or services. In fact, some businesses spend up to fifty percent of their revenues on advertising and marketing expenses. Rather than spending their money in traditional advertising, such as newspaper and magazine ads, broadcast ads and phone books, some network marketing companies choose to share their money with their best customers. The best customers are people who value the product or services and can't keep from telling others about it. Paying valued customers a referral fee or commission is less expensive and word of the valuable products and services spreads more efficiently.

When I'm happy with a product or service, I find it hard to keep my mouth shut about it. Why would I want to? If what you have or know will benefit others, then why wouldn't you want to tell them about it? Marketing research shows people prefer to do business with people they know. They also prefer to use products and services people they know have already found to be valuable. As a business owner, I'd much rather reward my happy customers for spreading the word about my services than throw money into media campaigns that might or might not succeed.

If you can find a home-based business with a product or service you believe in and are passionate about, then it makes sense to consider representing it. The start-up cost for many of these businesses is low when compared to starting a traditional business. That's a huge bonus right there. Little start-up cost and low overhead eliminate one of the most difficult aspects of any business. In addition, the tax advantages of a home-based business give you a chance to save thousands of dollars each year in taxes—legally. That reason alone is a very compelling reason to start your own business.

I always keep my eye out for attractive home-based businesses. I love the concept, and believe that if done properly and with tact, anybody can benefit greatly from the right opportunity. Many people will enjoy your excellent products and services, and the value provided to the marketplace will multiply. In choosing a home-based business, just remember—the product or service you choose must be one you feel passionately about and know you'll benefit from, too.

What about an additional income stream? Many people make significant income with this concept, too. I know quite a few people who make great money through network marketing. The best opportunities are those that involve your passions. Spreading the word about something you value and are sure other people need can come naturally. With technology, it has become exponentially easier to share your product or services with others worldwide. With consistent effort, the income stream begins to grow. Before you know it, you'll see people join your distribution network.

Network marketing allows you to take advantage of the awesome power of leverage. With the right product, the right business and compensation structure, it's possible to grow an income stream that will take on a life of its own. You can work hard, and expend effort over a period of time, then arrive at the point where you get paid over and over for the work you did up front. Is this a "Get Rich Quick" scheme? No way. Some of the most honest, conscientious and hard-working people I know are network marketing millionaires. They got there by working hard over a sustained period of time, providing value to an ever-expanding number of people. Now, that truly is a win-win scenario.

How do I choose a network marketing company?

We've discussed the benefits associated with network marketing. The right company, the right product, the right commission structure and minimal risks combine to make a winning combination. I've kept my eyes open, looking for such a "perfect combination" for years. I finally found one that's an ideal fit for me. The products and business platform are things I'm passionate about . In fact, when I discovered it, I almost couldn't believe it. Let me explain.

I had previously been involved with three network marketing companies. Each had tremendous products that I was passionate about that provided value to me and many people. I actually enjoyed good success and became a leader with all of them. However, all three of them were relatively new start ups with a "ground floor" opportunity. I almost cringe now when I hear those words. It takes an enormous amount of capital, market expertise, leadership, and a fail-proof duplication model for a network marketing company to stand the test of time.

All three of these companies I involved myself with went out of business. Current research shows that a new start up network marketing company has over a ninety percent chance of failure within five years. I have ZERO intention of ever joining a start up network marketing company and would caution you against that as well. I am only interested in building long term residual network marketing income. I want to maximize the chances that my hard work will pay off in residual income for many years after I have built it.

I hope by now you recognize network marketing as a legitimately powerful way to build wealth. Now it's time to choose a business that's right for you. There are so many companies out there that claim to have the best product or service and the best business opportunity. However, you want to be certain you are getting into the best one for you.

Let's step back and analyze the situation. Here are some interesting numbers. There have been nearly 60,000 network marketing companies start since the late 1950's and yet there are less than 1,000 operating today. Only eleven have made it to a billion dollars in annual sales and one of those is out of business. No wonder some people have reservations about the industry.

So why is it that not one of the network marketing companies that have started in the last 20 years can make it to a billion dollars in annual sales? Their compensation plans are supposed to be better and they all offer ground floor excitement, yet ninety percent are out of business or declining in sales after the initial surge. And, even when one does reach 250 million in sales they typically struggle mightily to hold the attention of their people and their numbers decline.

If you take the emotion out of it how would you select a company? Why not approach it like a professional business analyst and ask the hard questions? You want to look at the credit score, cash assets, budget for R&D and innovation, proof that the compensation plan works long term. You want to consider legal status regarding regulatory compliance, international presence and reputation, trademarks, unique products, corporate and field leadership, innovative technology, and a solid plan to keep things moving forward. Most importantly, what is the company's strategy to keep it solid so it won't fall like the others? Strive to find these answers regarding the company you consider joining.

Is it possible to have the excitement of a ground floor opportunity without the risks associated with many new start up companies that claim to be the next billion dollar company with little chance of ever delivering? The answer is yes. I have found the perfect company for me. My income from network marketing is rapidly becoming one of my best business income streams. I believe my income from my network marketing company may eventually surpass all of my other business venture incomes combined. That excites me! Do your research and find the perfect company for you. If I can be of assistance to you in your search and evaluation of a company, feel free to e-mail me at drclark@ beatingallodds.com. I will do my best to help you.

DailySuccessStream

"Self education will make you a fortune"
— Jim Rohn

In July of 2009, I was awarded the Young Entrepreneur of the Year Award by the Boise Metro Chamber of Commerce. Shortly afterward, the chamber asked me to speak at an event for local business owners and chamber members. They asked me to share the secrets to my exciting business success during and despite the worst global recession since the Great Depression. My answer? DailySuccessStream. Let me explain.

I've been out of dental school for nearly seven years. As I've already said, I learned early on about the importance of continuing education. After summoning the courage to invest six thousand dollars and attend the business training program for dentists, I became a believer in putting money into education. Alone, it's not possible to learn everything there is to know. No one could live that long! Instead, we have the opportunity to fill in our minds with the knowledge of experts who are ready to share their wisdom and experience with us. We have a rare chance for these greats to teach us what they know. In other words, we can learn from the mistakes of those who have gone before us to achieve success—despite those mistakes. When I invest (notice I didn't use the word "spend") money in business, motivational or other self-improvement education, I always get a return on my investment. It's not uncommon to have a return of ten times or greater. So, a return on investment of 10:1 means I invest one dollar and end up with ten dollars in return. I'll play that game all day long!

The more you learn, the more you earn—and you can take that to the bank! It's true. There's so much important and new information available—it's all but impossible to keep up by yourself in today's "You snooze; you lose" society. It pays to find and connect with information you need that's specific to your interest, career or passion. By learning from the experts, you'll have what it takes to soar to higher levels of success over a shorter time. Learning on a continuing basis will keep your mind sharp, help you think clearly and recognize how to turn mundane situations into opportunities. Lucrative opportunities surround us, no matter what the economy is doing. Without constant education, though, they may appear fuzzy and even remain invisible. With education, however, they become crystal clear, and we'll recognize them quickly.

Because I'm so focused on success and abundance, I often see opportunity when others think the sky is falling. In less than five years, I went from being a small one-dentist office to a two-doctor business, not to mention creating multiple streams of income that consistently produce. If one of those income streams has a weak month, it's no problem. The others compensate for it. None of this would have been possible if I hadn't been committed to filling my mind with the very best information available. My investment of thousands of dollars every year in ongoing learning is worth every penny. Needless to say, I'm passionate about personal development because it pays very well—and not just monetarily.

You say, "Okay, Dr. Clark. That's all fine and good. But what if I don't have thousands of dollars to shell out on this self-education stuff?"

I realize that's a problem and it's bothered me in the past. I've thought about how great our world could be if everybody had access to the seminars and material I have. The fact that it can cost thousands of dollars to acquire this material literally excludes a large number of people—and they're most likely people who would benefit from it most. Then you add the cost of flights, hotels and other travel expenses to course tuition and materials. Believe me, it adds up fast! I've often wondered, "If people can't afford to pay for this education, then how will they get ahead?" Dentists have easier access to the funds necessary for many of these growth and development materials because banks are eager to lend us money.

But what about everyone else? How is an employee (someone who isn't a business owner) who makes less than $30,000 a year supposed to get the education to rise above that income? I found the answer with DailySuccessStream.com. To my great surprise and excitement, I discovered DailySuccessStream.com brings the best education material in business, self-improvement, motivation and many other topics in personal growth and development to the public for a fraction of what I've paid over the past six years. Now I have access to more of the best educational information than ever. Best of all, I've saved thousands of dollars. The same opportunity is available to everyone now at an affordable monthly price.

What is DailySuccessStream?

DailySuccessStream (DSS) offers an online personal development library for entrepreneurs, business owners, salespeople, lifelong learners and others. It's also great for individuals, families and organizations that want to improve their lives in a variety of ways. This exciting organization will forever change the way we learn.

DSS provides members a portal to learning through full-screen, high-definition video streaming technology. This subscription-based library of knowledge provides access to many of the world's best minds and ideas in the field of personal growth and development, along with many other subjects. DSS is already becoming the largest e-learning, continuous learning organization in the world.

DSS brings you the street smarts, experience and intellectual property of the top authors, teachers, trainers, speakers, coaches and consultants in sales, marketing, management, motivation, business training, leadership, network marketing, entrepreneurship, tax and investment strategies, parenting, relationships, negotiating and more. Content is delivered via the latest technology through audios and HD video to your computer or mobile device.

DailySuccessStream Faculty

DSS offers content from many of the most successful experts and entrepreneurs in the world, including among many others:

Tony Alessandra

Bill Bartmann

Kevin Carroll

Jim Cathcart

Dan Clark

Stephen M.R. Covey

Dennis Deaton

Tom Feltenstein

Patricia Fripp

John Gray

Garrett Gunderson

Mark Victor Hansen

T.J. Hoisington

Chet Holmes

Don Hutson

Shep Hyken

Paul Martinelli

Ivan Misner

Terri Murphy

Steve Siebold

Hyrum Smith

Marsha Petrie Sue

Brian Tracy

Sam Silverstein

Mark Sanborn

Scott McKain

William R. Patterson

And we're always adding more of the world's best to our team as more top speakers, authors, coaches and entrepreneurs recognize the opportunities this education company presents.

DailySuccessStream Mission

As a founding member of DailySuccessStream, I am proud to share more about the organization and two of its primary goals:

1. To make you better at what you already do.

2. To make you more savvy.

DSS's first goal is to help you become better at what you already do. We want you to become a better mother, father, spouse, employee and employer—a better person in general. You will become a better salesperson, entrepreneur, network marketer, team builder, small-business owner and more. No matter what you do, you can always become better. Through DSS, you can achieve your goals faster and better than you would have thought possible. You can become better than you were through the top training and educational resources provided by DailySuccessStream.

For more information about DailySuccessStream, and how you can use it to become better and more profitable in your current business or career, visit: http://www.BeatingAllOdds.com or go to: http://www.dailysuccessstream.com and sign up using the promo code: drclarkspecial to receive your first 5 days FREE. You may also go directly to the sign up page to receive the same offer at: http://members.dailysuccessstream.com/sign-up/drclarkspecial.

SUMMARY

"From the neck down, you are worth what common labor will pay. From the neck up, there are no limits."
— Cliff Clark

My grandfather Cliff Clark taught me this most valuable business lesson shortly after I finished college. I know I am blessed to have been so richly tutored by him. In recent years, I've spent as much time as possible at his bedside. Today, he is ninety-one years young and mentally sharp as a tack. He has been a businessman all his life. From his life experiences alone, I've glimpsed countless ways we can go into business for ourselves.

If you're a business owner, I encourage you to examine your business. Search for ways to increase your value to the marketplace, which will result in increased profits.

For those of you who aren't business owners *yet*, I have to ask, "What's stopping you?" Now's the time! It's never been easier than today to start a home-based business. The first step, getting started, is the key to taking this important step toward beating the odds.

To all business owners, now's the time to take responsibility for your taxes. Your accountant is not responsible for your taxes. Mind your business because nobody else is going to do it. There are lots of resources to help you learn legally to reduce your taxes.

I'm excited about this because as I move forward, I know one of the most lucrative strategies for creating wealth. Maybe you already knew it, but I didn't. The strategy is to reduce your taxes to the legal minimum through owning a business. Donald Trump, Sam Walton and all the other multi-millionaires and ba-jillionaires all know this. I learned from Sandy Botkin that eighty-five percent of America's millionaires don't make a lot of money! As business owners, they simply save at least ten percent of what they make, live on the rest and reduce their taxes to the legal minimum.

Think about it. You *can* win through business ownership.

SECTION FOUR

ACHIEVE

CHAPTER 16

Expect the Best Every Time

"Aim high. In the long run, you hit only what you aim at.
Therefore, even though you may fail,
you're better off aiming at something high."
— Henry David Thoreau

Whether you believe it or not, whether you recognize it or not, you get what you expect. I don't think I can say it enough—because this principle is key for anyone who wants to beat the odds in life. Successful people from all walks of life understand this principle and use it to their advantage.

Recently, I attended a BYU football game with about 60,000 other fans. I don't remember a lot about the game other than what I saw on the back of a T-shirt worn by a young man a few rows ahead of me. The Thoreau quote I used to open this chapter caught my eye and I squinted to see what it said. Upon close observation, I realized I'd come across a definite "writer-downer." I took a receipt out of my wallet and quickly wrote it down.

Positive or negative, great or small, no matter what—you get what you expect in life. So why not expect the very best? Why settle for mediocrity? This is a strong component of the Law of Attraction. What we focus on expands. Set your sights high and expect the best in all areas of life and you'll have the best chance to attract the right people, resources and circumstances to see your expectations become a reality.

You've probably been advised to save for a "rainy day," right? I've certainly heard it many times. T. Harv Eker teaches us to use extreme caution if we must think about negative events in the future, such as that dreaded "rainy day." Of course, we're all subject to setbacks and adversity, but we don't have to focus on them. It's great to be prepared, but we don't have to focus on rainy days, even while we're preparing for them. Instead, we can simply set aside adequate resources to draw upon should we ever need them, and remain focused on success and abundance at the same time! Because if we focus on rainy days, we tend to get them!

On the other hand, thinking about success and abundance puts us in line for pleasant events. Our thoughts lead to our expectations, which in turn become our realities. So instead of thinking about saving for a "rainy day," think about saving for financial independence. By focusing on financial independence, we have the best chance to achieve it. And if we have a rainy day along the way (everyone does), then we'll see it as nothing more than a speed bump on our road to success.

HENRY FORD'S EXPECTATION

Have you had a time when you've ever wanted to do something that, as far as you know, has never been done before? Let me ask that question a little differently to see if you answer the same way. Has there been a time when you decided to do something you knew had never been done before? Desire is the first and most important element to accomplishment. It precedes a definite decision to take action—to getting it done!

I love Napoleon Hill's story about Henry Ford in Hill's classic book, *Think and Grow Rich*. Millions of people think of Henry Ford as being lucky, a genius or extraordinary. However, Ford was just an ordinary person who expected extraordinary things. One of his biggest secrets was his ability to expect the best and not back down until it became a reality. He knew if he expected the best, he could get the best.

More than eighty years ago, Ford decided to do something that had never been done before. He decided to produce a V-8 motor with all eight cylinders cast in one block. He gathered his team of expert engineers and told them to produce it. Unanimously, they told him it wouldn't be possible to cast in one block. It had never been done before. Ford answered, "Build it anyway." Ford went back and forth with his engineers, and kept getting the same response, for more than a year. Through it all, Ford never lowered his expectation. He expected to achieve his vision, even though everyone thought it was impossible.

Finally, the engineers approached Ford one last time and declared the task impossible. He told them to stick to the task until they got it done, no matter how long it took. The engineers knew they'd have to keep at it and try to meet Ford's expectation in order to keep their jobs. So they did the only thing they could do. They went back to the drawing board and, as if by magic, the solution appeared and the entire block was cast in one piece. Ford had expected the best and in the end, he got it.

What eight-cylinder blocks would you like to produce in your life? As you look at your own life and the progress you've made toward your goals, you can empower yourself by expecting the best every time. Obviously, it takes firm resolve to persevere when you're making little, if any, progress. But the natural laws governing the universe favor those who plan to win, prepare to win and expect to win in life—and they're the people who usually do win.

THE WORLD'S BEST COOKIE

"Good enough never is."
— Debbi Fields

Just thinking about this subject makes my mouth water! When I was a teenager, my friends and I frequently took the bus into town to the mall. And every time we passed the Mrs. Fields Cookies store, I couldn't help but wander over to check out those world-famous cookies in the glass display case. The aroma alone could stop anyone in his tracks—and it usually did! I was no different than other people in the mall. It was just too hard to resist; I had to buy a cookie and eat it on the spot.

I recently read an article where Debbie Fields shared her secret for making such mouthwatering cookies. Her philosophy is, "Good enough never is."

"Who wants a good cookie if you can bite into one that's delicious and mouthwatering?" she asked. She expects the best and won't settle for anything less. She knows if her cookies are the best, then her company will be at the top. "There is always competition," Fields says. "Whatever you do, there will be competition. You have to decide how you're going to play. For me, I have to be the very best."

Debbi Fields believes what all successful people do. If you make the best product or offer the best service, then you have no reason to fear your competition. If you expect the best and become the best in your field, then the money will find you. Fields took her cookies to the extreme. She wasn't satisfied with producing a good cookie. She pushed the envelope to make the best cookie she could possibly make. She tested her recipe to see how much butter and chocolate she could put in before the dough would not hold anymore.

Once Fields created the "ideal" mouthwatering cookie, she didn't stop. She set the bar as high as it could go. Mrs. Fields cookies had to be warm and just out of the oven. Any cookies that sat on the shelf for more than two hours were donated to charity. No wonder I couldn't resist those cookies when I was a kid—and even today! And I'm not alone. Today, you'll find Mrs. Fields cookie franchises around the world, and if there's not one near you, you can get your "fix" online!

A TRUE CHAMPION

In 1968, a young man named George Foreman won the Olympic gold medal in boxing. This became the slingshot that propelled him into the world of professional boxing. He continued to succeed until he became the world heavyweight boxing champion. Then, at age twenty-seven, he hung up his gloves and left boxing.

After being away from boxing for ten years, Foreman had an itch to make a comeback. At age thirty-seven, he made a commitment to do what had never been done. Heavy, out of shape and pushing forty, Foreman knew he would have to give an extraordinary performance. He couldn't just be good; he had to expect to see the best in himself. "In time, I'll be champ of the world," he promised himself.

When the media learned of his decision to make a comeback for the boxing title, they mocked him early and often. Foreman learned to block out the negativity and skeptical comments about his goal.

"I don't hear the negatives anymore." — George Foreman

He started at rock bottom and took any fights he could get. When he entered the ring, he fought like it was for the championship of the world. Win after win, success after success, the skeptics began to disappear. George Foreman expected the best from himself. He was only content after he had given it all he had.

Finally at the creaky "old" age of forty-five, George Foreman earned his shot at the title. In November 1994, he achieved what many had declared impossible. He recaptured the title and became the heavyweight champion of the world. All the while, Foreman saw himself as someone who could conquer adversities. Today, he is no different. He is one of the most successful business entrepreneurs in the world. There is a pattern with all successful people. They expect to seize what they are reaching for and they most often get it.

Seeing the Invisible

"Only those who can see the invisible can achieve the impossible."
— Patrick Snow

A good friend of mine, Patrick Snow, is an international best-selling author, international speaker and small business consultant. Impressive credentials, I would have to agree! But it wasn't always this way for him. In fact, Patrick Snow struggled for years to find his niche in the corporate world. He had several jobs as he made his way along the bumpy road to success. Finally, Patrick realized working for someone else means you'll never have job security. He also knew an employer couldn't give him the lifestyle he wanted. To Snow, it's always family first. His wife, Cheryl, is a prosecuting attorney who works very hard to put abusive individuals behind bars. Patrick supports her mission to make the world a safer place. At the same time, he is committed to bringing up his two boys in the best possible environment.

After years of effort working for different employers, Patrick's vision was born. He set his sights high. He was going to have his proverbial cake and eat it, too. If he could work from home as a business consultant and be a professional speaker on a limited basis, then he could be around to help raise his boys. Patrick saw the invisible and left the corporate world for good. He was determined to succeed as an author, professional speaker and business consultant. It was anything but easy, but he stuck to it. He expected the best and today he is getting the best.

He was featured on the cover of a *USA Today* article titled "More Americans Put Families Ahead of Work." Snow has increased his income working from home. In fact, he is doing better now financially than he ever did with a "J-O-B." Not long ago, I spoke with Patrick about his success. He insists he's no genius, not even close. He says he's just a normal guy like anyone else. The only difference was his vision of expecting the very best. He didn't stop until he'd achieved his vision and goals—and he hasn't stopped! His desire to succeed professionally *and* be there for his family is a continuing reality.

SUMMARY

As you move forward, it's important to remember you can increase your chances of beating the odds by expecting the best. Whatever you want to accomplish, set your sights high and expect the outcomes you seek. The "how" is not really important here. What's important is your vision and commitment to do—and achieve—your very best. If you remain determined and know what to expect, the magic will happen. People, events and circumstances tend to conspire not *against*—but *for* the person—who expects the best every time.

CHAPTER 17

See Enthusiasm Work for You

"Life's blows cannot break a person whose spirit is warmed at the fire of enthusiasm."
— Norman Vincent Peale

In 2008, a dental consultant invited me to be a presenter at a two-day event for his top national clients. He set aside ninety minutes for me to talk about my dental assisting school and the opportunity I offer to dentists nationwide. I was set to be the last presenter at the end of a long first day. I didn't know if that would be good or bad.

When it was time for me to speak, about eleven hours had passed since the seminar started that morning. As I stood on stage and looked at the audience of dentists and their employees, I knew I had some serious work ahead of me. I knew they'd had it and sensed they weren't looking forward to hearing from a thirty-four year-old "kid." After all, I was one of the youngest dentists in the room—and some were close to twice my age. As I scanned the audience, I saw people with that familiar body language—the arms folded, disinterested "What's this kid going to teach me?"—posture. I watched as a few of them walked out before I ever said a word.

I wasn't intimidated by any of it. If anything, I was excited because I had a secret and I was sure it would work to my benefit. I'd used this secret before with consistently positive results.

I want to share my strategy before I continue the story. It's very simple:

Your level of enthusiasm will compensate for almost any deficiency.

That's right! As simple as it sounds, your enthusiasm will work to your benefit in almost any situation. Whatever you do, always do your best and do it enthusiastically.

Why? Enthusiasm is contagious and enthusiastic people are quite fortunate. It brings out powerful and positive emotions in others. If you're in sales, then be excited about your product. If you provide a service, then be excited about that service. People use emotions, more than logic, to make decisions. So your enthusiasm could mean the difference between a negative or positive outcome.

Now I'll get back to my story. I knew my product could provide a benefit to most every dentist in the room that day. Likewise, I knew it made sense for everyone to buy. Even though it made sense from a logical standpoint, I knew those doctors had to feel as excited about my product as I did. That's where enthusiasm took over.

The first five minutes on stage were the most important for my success. I began with an opening activity I knew would grab their interest. I gave it all the enthusiasm I had—and then some! Within ten minutes, I watched as arms unfolded, scowls turned into smiles and even those who'd been sulking and disinterested moved to the edges of their seats. I had 'em and I knew it! The rest of my enthusiastic presentation was a breeze!

Did I face any challenges going in? Sure! The odds were stacked against me from the get-go. People were tired. They'd heard sales pitches all day—a long eleven hours—and had made other purchases. I was young and many perceived me as having little experience. None of that mattered—it was Enthusiasm (with a capital E) to the rescue!

Do you wonder how the presentation ended? Well, after a talk that lasted about eighty minutes, I wrapped things up. Then, to my delight, people walked to the front of the room with their order forms complete, and handed them to me before I'd even finished speaking! My enthusiasm, combined with a great product, got the momentum started. Before I knew it, I was surrounded by "sold" dentists, all holding order forms. In the end, I'd sold a costly product to nearly forty percent of the dentists in the room.

The momentum and enthusiasm helped me overcome the odds. It seemed I'd generated a buzz at the seminar. The next morning, one of the dentists who'd walked out the previous day, approached me with his order form. He'd heard about my product from the other doctors and their enthusiasm convinced him that he needed my product, too!

This is a simple example of how I used enthusiasm to my benefit. Now, will enthusiasm alone help you accomplish anything? No way. However, if you have enthusiasm, you'll certainly do everything better than if you don't have it. The message here is to get out there and do whatever it takes to build and show enthusiasm and passion for your product or service. Genuine enthusiasm is empowering, even in a room full of tired, bored and hungry dentists!

MOTIVATION IS THE KEY

Okay, if enthusiasm is so important, then what do you need to do to get it? I think the best way to answer that question is: You need to get, and stay, motivated!

When you're motivated, then you're excited and energized about the task in front of you. Have you ever heard someone speak, or read a book, listen to a CD program or watched a webinar that really got your blood pumping? I have and I'm sure you have, too. One thing I've noticed is those feelings of optimism and enthusiasm don't last forever. They come in spurts.

I love listening to motivational speakers and surrounding myself with inspirational material in many different forms. A few years ago, I went to an event that featured motivational speaker James Malinchak. After giving hundreds of motivational speeches, I'm sure he's heard something similar to what I felt—that the enthusiasm doesn't last. People complain, saying the motivational stuff isn't a big deal because it's only temporary.

I love James' response when someone asks about this issue. He simply asks these naysayers if they all took showers that morning. That grabs their attention, and everyone gives an affirmative response. Then he asks if any of them had taken a shower before that day. Again the responses are positive. Then he asks why they'd taken a shower that day since they'd taken one before. The answer is obvious and the cynics finally begin to "get it."

Motivation is the same as taking a shower. You must take frequent "mental booster showers," or your attitude will begin to stink. And what about your enthusiasm? Without your regular "mental booster showers," you can forget your enthusiastic attitude. It will be gone.

What fires you up? What gets you excited? What makes you tick and what gets you ticked? It might be a favorite song on the radio. It might be an audio program you've listened to over and over again. It might be a book, a mentor, a coach or just anything else that motivates you. Exposing yourself to a daily dose of motivation will help ensure your enthusiasm stays at a peak.

> **WOULD YOU LIKE A REGULAR DOSE OF MOTIVATION?**
> I invite you to join me on **Facebook**: Taylor Clark. I regularly
> share motivational insights there.

BATTERY CHARGER VS. BATTERY DRAINER

While I was in undergraduate school, Tom Tervort, a successful insurance salesman, recruited me to work with him. I didn't know a thing about life insurance and the retirement products available in the industry. Still, I gladly accepted his offer to train me to sell life insurance products. I figured the experience would help me understand the subject and raise my financial IQ.

I studied hard and passed my Series 6 and 63 Securities exams, along with the Life and Disability Exam for the State of Utah. Then, I hit the streets, eager to find prospects who would be happy for me to help them with their life insurance needs. It didn't take long to learn that a career in sales wasn't going to be a cakewalk. In fact, most of the time it was downright frustrating. I realized I had much to learn if I were going to overcome the zillion objections people used.

Tom met with his team weekly and left daily voice mail messages to help keep us plugged into the right mental attitude. Running into rejections and being turned down was not good on our enthusiasm gas tanks. Sometimes it seemed tempting just to give up and quit. Tom's meetings and daily messages did a lot to boost our morale when times were tough.

One day, Tom taught me something I've never forgotten. He said, "You can be a battery charger or you can be a battery drainer. Which type do you enjoy being with? Which one are you?" My answers to those questions were obvious. I wanted to be a battery charger all the time. But I have to admit it was easy to slip, become negative and turn into a battery drainer. Being a battery drainer—complaining, blaming and justifying—never felt good. And I certainly didn't want to be with a drainer!

Since then, in everything I do, I strive to be a battery charger. People who fall into this category are optimists who do whatever it takes to keep their enthusiasm tanks full. Salespeople in this category are the ones people like and choose to do business with. Good things happen to these people because they attract what it takes to achieve success.

With this new "battery charger" view of myself and others, I turned failure and discouragement into excitement and success. I enjoyed my work as a financial services salesman so much I was tempted to stay with it instead of going to dental school.

SYNERGY

One of the most important things you can do to generate enthusiasm is to be very careful in choosing whom you associate with. Get rid of the battery drainers and stick with the battery chargers. Think about the people you know who are always excited and enthusiastic. How do you feel when you're around them?

Personally, I choose to associate with one of my business partners, Dr. J.D. Drake of Idaho Falls, Idaho. A few years ago, Dr. Drake became one of my dental assisting school clients. He was enthusiastic from the start, and I knew his dental assisting school was going to be a great success. And I was surely correct! Before his first class even started, he'd generated such a buzz that the local news station got wind of it. They went to his office and did an incredible news story, which drove business his way. I found an enthusiasm gold mine with this guy!

I knew if I could team up with Dr. Drake more often, we could combine our enthusiasm in a synergistic way. I offered to give him a percentage of my business if he would join me as a business partner. This partnership has resulted in explosive growth, with Assist to Succeed programs continuing to open across the U.S.

Dr. Drake and I are business partners on multiple fronts now. His high level of enthusiasm helps keep my level of enthusiasm at its peak. We do this through phone calls, e-mails, text messages and attending business events together. Funny thing is, he probably thinks I'm the one with all the enthusiasm, and that keeps him motivated and excited continuously to hit it!

SUMMARY

Enthusiasm fuels the fire of success. You'll get further with any effort and goal if you approach it with enthusiasm. The right people, events, books, educational materials, career, organizations and actions will combine to determine how much enthusiasm you generate on any given day. So, during the day, be sure to check in and connect with your best sources of enthusiasm, whatever they may be. Doing so will increase your chances of beating the odds in any endeavor.

CHAPTER 18

Build Wealth on Any Income

"If you are not fully, totally and truly committed to creating wealth, then chances are you won't. "
— T. Harv Eker

This chapter is near and dear to me. I can't wait to tell you, and everybody I know, about the simple, yet powerful principles of creating wealth. These principles work for everyone, including you—regardless of how much money you make.

If you go out into the world and ask people how they plan to retire, you'll get the same response from nearly everyone. Most people are doing the same thing they think everyone else is doing. They're going to work, getting a paycheck, paying all the bills first and hoping they have something left to put into savings. But they're going about it all wrong; they're doing it backwards!

Why in the world would you want to pay everyone else first? Don't you work hard for your money? Why should other people get your hard-earned money before you do? Don't get me wrong here. I'm *not* talking about compromising your integrity by not paying your bills— not even close. What I *am* talking about is the most powerful strategy for accumulating wealth on the planet.

"A part of all you earn is yours to keep."
— George S. Clason, *The Richest Man in Babylon*

PAY YOURSELF FIRST

Pay yourself first. It's as simple as that. A portion of everything I earn is mine to keep. By the time I'd finished school and joined the workforce full-time, I'd heard about this concept many times. I first learned about it from my friend and mentor, Tom Tervort, a retirement products salesman. He stopped by my tiny student apartment one day when I was trying to get into dental school. I listened to him for about an hour and from that point forward, my life has never been the same. What he said sank in hard and has been a part of me since.

Tom shared his version of this vital "pay yourself first" principle of accumulating wealth. He said obviously I needed to pay God first in the form of tithing. I agreed with that since I believe in tithing and the divine rewards that come with it. By the way, the principle of tithing is not unique to those of my faith. The most financially successful people I know, either personally or through my studies, participate in tithing. I'll cover this in detail later.

Then, Tom explained I should pay myself second. "Pay God and yourself before anybody else gets a dime," he said. That was an eye-opener! Because while tithing wasn't new to me, the concept of paying myself first was. Tom told me to take a percentage of my income and consider it "gone." I should put that money in a place where I couldn't get to it—a place where it could produce more money—and then forget about it, because it was "gone."

I was skeptical. My initial thoughts were the same as those of everyone new to this concept. What if I don't have enough money to pay the bills? What if my car breaks down? What if I don't have enough money for groceries? Shouldn't I keep my whole paycheck in my bank account to make sure there's enough to pay all the bills?

NO! This is where the magic begins.

I'm going to use the same example Tom shared with me that day. "Taylor, suppose your car broke down today and no longer worked. What would you do?"

"I'd get it fixed. I need to have my car," I replied.

"Exactly! You'd either take money out of your bank account or find another way to get the money to get your car fixed," Tom said. "If you have money in your bank account, then you'd use that first."

That made sense because obviously I needed my car and would have to pay to get it repaired. Tom continued, "Okay. Now, suppose you'd been paying yourself first before your car broke down. That money is gone because you can't get to it, so you won't be using it. How are you going to get that car fixed?"

My reply was the same. "I would get my car fixed. I need to have my car!"

"Exactly! You'd go to your savings account and withdraw the money needed to fix your car—if you had enough money in your savings account, that is," Tom continued. "If there wasn't enough money in the bank, then you'd find a way to get it because you need your car. You'd take on an extra job, work extra hours, sell a useless knick-knack on e-Bay or something. The point is you'd do whatever it took to come up with enough money to get your car fixed. We all would. And the magic part is, we'd all go through the same process whether we'd been paying ourselves first or not."

Then the light went on. I knew exactly what Tom was talking about. I understood the vision he was sharing with me and I got excited.

Whether that ten percent was in my bank account or not, I knew I would find a way to get my car fixed. In other words, I realized that by paying myself first, I would find a way to live on the rest.

And there you have it. Every self-made millionaire and billionaire understands—and practices—this simple, yet powerful strategy.

MILLIONAIRES ARE BORING

Study after study reveals the characteristics of America's millionaires. One of my favorite books about millionaires is *The Millionaire Next Door* by Thomas Stanley and William Danko. The book contains the results of the authors' years of studying America's millionaires. It's an eye-opener for many people because it shows that most millionaires don't fit the stereotype; they're not the flashy and unapproachable people we picture them as being.

For the most part, millionaires are boring. They may be average people with average jobs or careers who live in modest homes. They live below their means. They always pay themselves first and live on the rest. The typical American millionaire could be your next-door neighbor and you wouldn't even know it! All millionaires understand, and live by, the following principle:

It's not what you make. It's what you keep that counts.

Income is relative and it's not as important as much as you might think. In fact, it might be easier for a laborer who earns $40,000 a year to accumulate wealth than for a surgeon who brings home $800,000 a year. The rubber meets the road when it comes to living at, or preferably below, your means. Wealth is what you accumulate. It's not what you make. Income is not as relevant as most people believe when it comes to creating wealth.

MAKE IT AUTOMATIC

You build extreme wealth by paying yourself first. Since this takes discipline, most people don't do it. Fortunately though, David Bach shares a sure-fire way to become wealthy. If you follow his strategy, you are guaranteed to become wealthy.

In Bach's book *Automatic Millionaire*, he teaches an easy way to ensure you'll get paid first: Make it automatic. Have your bank set up automatic withdrawal to take a certain amount or percentage from your income each month. You'll likely find it surprisingly easy to make do with the remaining money and stretch it to meet your needs. Meanwhile, money will go toward your nest egg each month—and you won't even miss it.

Getting along without the money you pay yourself is easier than you might think. When I tried it the first time, I was surprised to see I was able to pay the bills and take care of my family with what remained after paying myself. It didn't take long to get used to the money not being there. It's amazing how quickly you can arrive at the point of not missing it.

This automatic payment strategy works well with most everything, including short-term savings, house payments, car payments, college funds for the kids and more. Give it a try. Set up an automatic withdrawal from your bank account that will go directly to your nest egg. Then enjoy the feeling of empowerment as you see compounding interest work wonders for you.

YOUR GOLDEN GOOSE

Okay, you're paying yourself first. Now what? What are you supposed to do with the money? This money is directed to creating your very own golden goose, a goose that lays golden eggs for you.

The story of the legendary Golden Goose, which has been told for generations, comes from those classics we all grew up with—*Aesop's Fables.*

A man and his wife had the good fortune to possess a goose which laid a golden egg every day. Lucky though they were, they soon began to realize they were not getting rich fast enough. Imagining the bird must be made of gold inside, they decided to kill it. Then, they thought, they could obtain an entire store of precious metal at once. However, upon cutting the goose open, they found its innards were just like that of any other goose.

The foolish man realized he had destroyed his means of getting a golden egg each day by trying to get everything at once. He had killed his precious golden goose and with that, destroyed his steady income stream of golden eggs.

Now back to reality. As you watch while money begins to accumulate from your automatic self-payments, the following questions arise:

1. Do you reach a point at which you start to draw upon the interest earned and the principle?

2. Do you try to estimate how much longer you're going to live to make sure you'll never use all of your nest egg?

3. When do you spend that money?

The answer is…drum roll please…NEVER!

Why would you kill your golden goose?

If you discipline yourself to stick with your strategy, the time will come when your golden goose will have golden offspring. Then you'll have lots of geese laying dozens of golden eggs. The eggs are what you take. Most people don't have the discipline to reach this point—the point when wealth is within their reach. The ones who do reap the benefits follow the principles of wealth accumulation—principles that work for anyone.

KNOCKING OUT DEBT

Getting and staying out of debt is crucial to accumulating wealth. However, I don't want you to focus on this too much because what we focus on expands. By focusing on debt, we just attract the circumstances to keep us in debt and bring more debt. Instead, I'd like to share what I learned from Randy Davis, who has been a financial advisor to extremely prosperous clients. I heard him speak several years ago.

Now mind you, I was not even *close* to being wealthy enough to be one of Randy's clients. He does not hurt for business and only accepts clients who have reached a certain level of wealth. I had the opportunity to listen to the basic wealth accumulating strategies he shares with his clients. Even though some of it is counterintuitive and goes against traditional financial advice, I chose to follow it.

Randy's strategy was pretty simple. He suggested setting up automatic payments for all debts, including your home mortgage. Then take whatever you can scrimp together after meeting your living expenses and add that to the minimum payment on the debt with the **smallest** balance. Before long, that debt will be gone. Then take the amount you had been paying to the now-gone debt and apply it to the *next* smallest balance. Before long, that debt will be gone. Repeat the process with the next smallest balance until all your debts are gone, including your house.

Along the way, unexpected chunks of money may come in, especially as you remain focused on abundance rather than scarcity. Take those chunks and capture them. Apply them to your debt with the lowest balance to speed up the process. This really works! I've experienced it.

The real magic begins with what Randy calls the "Acceleration Margin." With all your debts erased, you have a huge chunk of money to throw into your golden goose fund. Put that money to work for you and start to generate residual or passive income. You'll literally begin making money when you sleep! Interest can be an empowering friend or a crushing enemy. I'll take the former over the latter any day of the week!

This formula, combined with frugal living, works wonders. For twelve years, Jannie and I lived conservatively and we still do. Our home is nice and sufficient for our needs. It's nothing fancy, though. I still drive my '95 Honda Civic that's in excellent condition—and of course, paid off. We often followed the mantra, "Fix it up, wear it out, make it do or do without." We tried never to spend money we didn't have and avoided consumer debt like the plague.

This simple formula works wonders. Following this strategy, we paid off all our debts—including student loans, dental practice loans, a minivan payment and even our mortgage! Getting rid of the house payment was the big one. I went against the advice of all the local "financial gurus." Several of them balked at my stubbornness not to strip the equity from my home and invest it. After all, the market was doing very well in 2005. These gurus had every answer in the book to counter my decision to pay off my home using Randy Davis' strategy.

Several years after implementing these strategies and sticking with them, we own our home and have no debt to go along with it. We reached this point just before the market took a nosedive. Today we are in a severe recession and people all around us are losing their homes, many from following the very advice I decided to shun. I can't tell you how happy and grateful I am that I was able to hear and learn from Randy Davis years ago. That guy changed my life and helped me get to where I am today.

WEALTH IS A MINDSET

Several years ago, I listened to an interview with multi-billionaire Bill Bartmann. Recently, I met Bill in person and spoke with him. Bill has been ranked as the twenty-fifth wealthiest person in America. He didn't get there by inheritance or luck, though. He grew up in poverty. His father was a janitor. He didn't get there because he's a genius either. He had trouble in school. Bill is very familiar with failure. In fact, Bill claims he has failed in more things than anyone he knows. What then, makes him so successful?

Bill had an extremely difficult experience as a young man. At seventeen years of age, he was hospitalized six months due to a fall that broke his back. During the time he was stuck in a hospital room, the only thing to read was a book called *Think and Grow Rich* by Napoleon Hill. Bill took the book and devoured it. In fact, he says he read that book 100 times because there was nothing else to do.

Bill says he learned that we all have control over basic things in life if we choose to exercise it. That book effectively taught Bill the incredible power we all have to use our marvelous minds. The lessons and principles in that book tell how to use your mind and thoughts combined with action to bring to pass powerful results in life. He learned how to acquire a success-conscious mindset that has helped him ever since. Incidentally, he learned how to set his first goal from reading that book. He decided he would walk out of that hospital despite the doctor's prognosis of paralysis. Six months later, he walked out on his own two feet.

That book by Napoleon Hill was a catalyst for Bill Bartmann. It taught him how to think big, set big goals and achieve them. The wealth and abundance mindset has served him very well ever since.

Bill Bartmann's success as a result of reading *Think and Grow Rich* is not unique. I can't tell you how many times I have heard about, read about or listened to many extremely wealthy people tell how they did it. The thing most of them tend to have in common is that it all began with Napoleon Hill's classic book. It took Hill more than twenty years to accumulate his study of the wealthiest people of his time. Through it, he discovered many universal principles of success and wealth that govern the universe, principles that will work for anyone who chooses to use them.

SUMMARY

I hope the great news in this chapter has encouraged you. You can become wealthy, no matter how much money you make. Of course, it may come faster with greater income, but the same principles will work regardless.

The encouraging thing is that no matter who you are, no matter how old you are, no matter how financially upside-down you may be today, you can decide today to do something about it. The really exciting part is that when you follow these universal principles for accumulating wealth, then implement them, and take consistent action with them, the financial picture can change very, very quickly.

Money isn't everything. I realize that. However, it is a very important part of life. I have had it and I have not had it. I'll tell you what—I'd rather have it any day. As Zig Ziglar teaches, money ranks right up there in importance with oxygen. If we can accumulate great wealth, we can give more freely of our time, talents and resources to the noble causes that are near and dear to our hearts. Without it, we are limited in the good we can do in this world.

It's my hope that everyone who reads this book can eventually reach the point in life where he or she no longer has to worry about finances. No more worrying about how the bills are going to get paid. No more wondering what the next paycheck is going to be. My hope for you is that you can create financial independence so you can serve your family and humanity in the best possible way, without having financial limits.

CHAPTER 19

Lead the Way

"Leadership is the ability to decide what has to be done,
and then get people to want to do it. "
— General Eisenhower

WHAT IS A LEADER?

A leader is a member of a group or organization of more than one person who effectively induces others to take action toward a specific purpose. A leader of a family can be a responsible father, a loving mother, a wise grandparent and so on. A leader of a company could be the CEO, vice president of sales or any standout team member who can consistently influence the others to act. Leaders sometimes come with an official title or in some cases, have no title at all. Great leaders all have certain characteristics in common.

I remember an event that took place in 1981 when I was eight years old. My mother was glued to the television, watching a wedding being televised live on one of the local channels. At the time, I wondered what the big deal was. All I saw was some lady wearing a fancy white dress with a very long train that followed quite a ways behind her. I had no idea who she was. Today, I know it was Princess Diana, one of the most influential leaders who ever lived.

"The true measure of leadership is influence;
nothing more, nothing less."
— John C. Maxwell

John Maxwell sheds some light on Princess Diana's leadership qualities in his book, *The 21 Irrefutable Laws of Leadership.* Diana was a former kindergarten teacher and seemed overwhelmed by all the attention she received when she married Prince Charles of England. Almost one billion people around the world watched the televised wedding ceremony that July day. Though Diana at first seemed uncomfortable with the spotlight, she quickly took advantage of it as she rallied the public to support good causes.

While Diana's husband, Prince Charles, had the wealth, royalty status and position, it was Diana who intrigued the world. People couldn't seem to get enough of her. Why? Maxwell says Diana was a master of influence. She made things happen. For the sixteen years following her marriage, her popularity increased greatly as did her influence. She won over the world. In fact, in a 1996 London poll, Diana was voted as the number one most caring person in the world. Mother Teresa came in second. What a great indication of her influence on people!

In 1997, the world was shocked to learn of the horrible automobile accident that took her life. Diana's leadership was so strong that even after death, she continued to influence many people. Her funeral was broadcast on radio and television in more than forty languages. NBC estimated that more than twice the number of people who watched her wedding watched her funeral. This can only be because she was a strong leader who influenced people on a global scale.

Great leaders do not necessarily have wealth, status or position. In fact, one of the most powerful leaders ever was Mahatma Gandhi. He was small in stature, did not have wealth and wore the most minimalist of clothing. Yet, he was one of the most powerful men of all times, most notably because of his ability to unite a country. Through his words and deeds, Gandhi influenced more than 200 million people to cooperate and unite in causes of non-violence and conflict resolution.

Think of some great leaders you know, or have known, personally. What makes you think of them as leaders? Whoever they are, they probably inspire you. Maybe you see them as selfless individuals committed to a worthy cause. They effectively move you to take action toward a specific purpose. Great leaders get everyone in an organization to believe in a specific dream. Leaders come in many forms. A leader may be a parent, a church leader, a co-worker, a friend or a business associate. No matter where you find them, good leaders follow universal principles of leadership to achieve consistent results.

A LEARNABLE SKILL

Achieving results through the efforts of others is not the same as trying to do it all yourself. Good leaders understand the principles behind good leadership. They learn these principles, put them into practice and seek ways to improve as time goes on. Good leaders understand that their ability to induce others to do what needs to be done is important to the organization's success.

Every organization depends on good leadership for success, whether the leader is appointed or just emerges. The good news is most leaders are made, not born. Experts tell us that leadership is a learnable skill and, to a degree, can be acquired by just about anyone.

Peter Drucker, known by many as the father of modern management, was once asked whether it was possible to be a natural leader. I love his response because it gives me hope. Perhaps it will do the same for you. He said there may be natural leaders, but with so few of them in the world, they really make no difference in the greater scheme of things.

THE SECRETS OF LEADERSHIP

If you want to become a better leader, then I recommend John C. Maxwell's book *The 21 Irrefutable Laws of Leadership*. Maxwell promises if you follow these laws, people will follow you.

I love the seven secrets of leadership, as taught by one of my great mentors, Brian Tracy. He explains that any organization's success—including your family—is determined by your ability to lead. As one of the world's experts on leadership, Brian also teaches that leadership can be learned. Though there are countless books, tapes and educational programs out there on leadership, I'm going to focus now on Tracy's Seven Leadership Keys, the "Seven C's."

The first key is clarity. You need to be clear about what you're doing. What are you trying to accomplish? It's like trying to get somewhere. You're more likely to get there if you know where you're headed.

The second key is competence. The future belongs to those who are good at what they do. The best in any particular field will do what it takes to keep getting better. Studies reveal that the top twenty percent in any field typically earn five to ten times more than the rest. Why? Because they're good at what they do and keep getting better. The secret to competence is understanding that there is no status quo. You're either growing or you're dying. It's impossible just to stay right where you are. If you don't commit to excellence in your field, then you simply will default to mediocrity.

The third key is constraints. Have you set goals but been unable to reach them? What's holding you back? What obstacles and constraints are out there? If you take a close look at your constraints, those things that are holding you back, you'll find eighty percent of them are internal. Internal constraints are factors you can control and do something about right now. Only twenty percent of constraints are external and beyond your control—the economy, the presiding government, the weather, etc.

The fourth key to good leadership is creativity. Good leaders always search for ways to do things faster, better and, if possible, at a better cost. In any endeavor, problems and challenges arise. You can choose to focus on the problems or to focus on the solutions. Brian Tracy says each of us is a potential genius. To become a genius, he says you must become solution-oriented. Focus your thoughts and attention on solutions most of the time. As you do this, you will exercise your creativity more. Like a muscle that gets stronger with use, you will become more creative as you use your creativity more.

The fifth leadership key is continuous learning. You've heard it before and you'll hear it again. The more you learn, the more you earn. As we've discussed, we become what we allow to enter our minds. Seek learning and wisdom from the best books. Protect what you permit to enter your mind. If you are not getting better through continuous education, you are getting worse. Become a life-long learner.

The sixth key is concentration. Today, there's so much out there competing for our attention. Many times it's the good things that truly keep us from the great things. Put your full focus on one thing at a time. On any given day, choose the most important key task to complete and work on it. Do not leave it until it's 100 percent done. I love what Zig Ziglar's mother taught him when he was a youngster. She said, "Once the task you have begun, leave it not until it's done."

The seventh key is commitment. I hear this from the experts on a regular basis. Be totally committed to what you do. When it's time to work, then get to work. Get rid of distractions that would break the momentum you create at work. A good example is that cell phone. Many cell phones alert you when you get a text message, e-mail message or other messages in addition to the actual phone call. Ask yourself, "Can all of this wait?" If so, then turn it off and work. Don't get on the Internet or give your attention to any interruption that is not in line with the task at hand.

I want to talk about the flip side of the work coin. When it's time to play, then it's time to play! When you go on a family vacation, be 100 percent with your family. Don't shortchange your spouse and kids. I recently went to Disneyland and saw something that bothered me. A guy was there with his wife and kids. He might have been with his family physically, but in reality, he was at work—on his cell phone doing business—ignoring his family. Why even bother to take a family vacation if those most important in your life don't get your time and attention? Something cool happens when you focus on your family during family time and play during playtime. You get the rest and rejuvenation you need to fill your energy gas tank. Then, when it's time to get back to work, you're ready to hit it hard and go after it. Even better, you'll build family memories to last a lifetime.

I'm going to add one leadership key to Brian's Seven C's. A good leader consistently takes action. Become and remain a person of action. Be decisive and act on your objectives. People respect and follow a person who takes action. Action-takers send out signals to potential followers that they know what they're doing and where they're going. We all naturally gravitate toward the person who takes action.

A NEST OF EAGLES

Now that we have identified the characteristics of a good leader, can you think of a person who influenced you as a youngster? I can. When I was young, I was actively involved in scouting. When I turned eleven, I was fortunate to move into the troop of one of our area's greatest scout leaders. He had a reputation of excellence and was becoming legendary in our city. His name is Jim Yardley. As I look back on my scouting experience, I can see why he was so successful with so many boys. He influenced us through using leadership principles.

Trying to lead a group of teenage boys is like trying to herd cats. It's not an easy task! But Jim Yardley was an expert at it. Inspired by his leadership, I was consistently motivated to work hard toward my ultimate goal in scouting. I wanted to earn my Eagle Scout award and so did all the other boys in my large troop. The big day came shortly after my fourteenth birthday. During a Court of Honor, I was presented with the Eagle Scout award. A fourteen-year-old Eagle Scout? Anybody in scouting knows how impressive that is.

As much as I'd like to claim brilliance and credit for reaching this high goal at such an early age, the credit goes to Jim Yardley for his masterful leadership. Most of the other boys earned their Eagles, too, and many did it at a young age. Lots of boys in our neighborhood consistently entered the troop as the older ones left. For years, Jim led each group and achieved the same results. In fact, to this day I don't know of another scout leader who has helped more boys achieve one of scouting's highest honors.

As a result of his great leadership, Jim Yardley created a nest of Eagles. Each one has gone out into the world and is doing much good. Through his leadership, Jim left a legacy that the next generation is repeating with their boys. As I look back on those who benefited from his leadership, I am amazed at what they have become today. Doctors, dentists, scientists, corporate leaders, business owners, teachers, trainers, an author, community and church leaders, fathers and many others will praise his name forever.

SUMMARY

Good leadership is what makes a good organization great. One of the best examples of "good to great" was demonstrated by two brothers named Dick and Maurice. The brothers started a small hamburger restaurant in Southern California. Their business grew and became very popular. Profits soared until they reached a plateau. The brothers became very wealthy for a time. However, the business failed to continue its growth until a man named Ray Kroc came along.

Ray Kroc took over the restaurant and introduced his vision for what it could become. He developed a pattern of business that was systematic and could be duplicated. His system was designed to work anywhere in California, or the rest of the world for that matter. Kroc's little hamburger restaurant grew into what many consider to be the most successful business in the world! Today, McDonald's restaurants dot the globe and billions upon billions of people have been served there. What a great example of what good leadership can do for any organization!

This world is a better place because of the many great leaders who inhabit it. It will continue to become a better place as people seek to learn and implement the universal laws of leadership. And they're yours for the taking. If you want to become more successful in any endeavor, then you have to become a better leader. The most important person you will ever lead will be yourself. Once you accomplish that, then you'll open up the door to lead others. You will be able to beat the odds much faster and easier as you effectively enlist the help of others. People will rally to your cause as you exercise good leadership. They will see the benefits in helping you get what you want because you in turn will be helping them get what they want.

CHAPTER 20

Achieve More With Focus

"Concentrate all your thoughts upon the work at hand. The sun's rays do not burn until brought to a focus."
— Alexander Graham Bell

One day when I was a young boy, a neighborhood friend introduced me to a magnifying glass and taught me how to use it. I know what you're thinking. Little boys and a magnifying glass are typically not a good combination. I can assure you, though, we didn't set any houses on fire.

We went out to the driveway that sunny summer day. My friend showed me how the magnifying glass works. We gathered some dead, dry leaves and took them to the sidewalk. I was amazed at what I saw as he focused the sun's rays to a tiny point. It didn't take long for that leaf to start smoking and burn. When I tried it, I noticed how the sun passed through the glass and made a circle of light on the leaf. I made the circle big and I made it small. I was most amazed at how small I could make it. I burned lots of leaves. Then I decided to put my own hand under the glass to see how long I could stand it. I'll tell you, once that circle of light became a tiny dot, it really hurt fast!

Focus will magnify the rays of effort in all work we engage in. Like setting fire to a dry leaf in seconds, an intense focus will light the fuse to the progress bomb. I learned the principle of focus at an early age.

However, I'm still learning today how extremely powerful focus can be. I often find myself amazed at the results of engaging in activities of intense focus over periods of time.

Me write a book? Are you kidding? That's what I used to think. I never thought about putting myself in the category of "author"—at least at first. Yet, writing this book has become one of the most enjoyable and surprisingly achievable things I've ever done. The key for me is to set aside pockets of focused time, dedicated to writing. I turn off the phone, close the office doors, put on inspirational music and write. The more I can tune everything out, the more I'm able to get in a "zone." I'm amazed at how fast the pages accumulate with focused efforts of two to three hours at a time.

AN AIRPLANE LESSON

As a wholesale produce businessman, my father frequently took trips to the fields where the growers produced the fruits and vegetables. One day when I was about thirteen years old, my dad invited me to go with him to California. We flew from Utah to California and met the owner of Agri-Sales, one of the companies my father did business with. Many of these wholesale produce owners use small airplanes to fly to their different fields.

The pilot, my dad, my sister and I boarded a small airplane and headed down the California coast into Baja, Mexico. We landed on a flat dirt runway in what seemed to be the middle of nowhere. We got out and were shown huge strawberry fields where scattered groups of workers packed strawberries into strawberry flats and loaded them into an air-cooled semi truck.

After spending time in the fields and filling ourselves with all the big, juicy red strawberries we could eat, we headed back to the plane. The pilot turned to me and said, "You are going to fly us back." I didn't think much of it until it was time to board the plane. He wasn't kidding! As we approached the plane, he motioned for me to jump into one of the two pilot seats. The plane was dual controlled and could be navigated from either the right or the left seat.

The pilot explained that he would take care of take-off and then turn it over to me once we reached cruising altitude. As I sat there, I was amazed at all the gauges, knobs, switches and controls for such a little airplane. After we were airborne, he gave me a lesson on how to go up, down, right and left.

As I looked through the cockpit window, all I saw was brown terrain in every direction. Everything looked the same. How in the world was I supposed to keep us going in the right direction? The pilot provided the answer to that question. He explained that I needed to look out at the horizon as far as I could see and focus on one thing. Once I had something to look at, then I needed to keep focused on that object until we got close to it. Then I was to repeat the process: look out into the horizon again and find the next thing to focus on. Repeat this process until we get to our destination.

Life is a lot like that plane ride. We first need to know what we want or where we are going. We need somebody to show us how to get there. Once we know what we need to do, we need to stay focused on our objective. The better the focus, the straighter the line our path of travel will be toward our goal.

If we wander and get off course, we do not need to turn the plane around and start over. We simply refocus on our point on the horizon and head back toward it. Pilots of large commercial airliners will tell you they seldom fly in one perfectly straight line from one place to another. In reality, the path of travel is more of a zigzag pattern. The fewer the zigs and zags, the faster the airplane gets there. The more focused we can be, the straighter and shorter our path of travel to success will be.

BORN WITHOUT ARMS

"All things are within reach."
— John Foppe

Can you imagine not having any arms? How would you get yourself dressed or drive a car? How would you open a can of soda or cook breakfast? How would you write, draw or read a book? How would you comb your hair or play the trombone? How would you shave or put on your watch? How would you do anything?

John Foppe is an incredible individual. He was born without arms. From day one, he has faced unique obstacles to living a normal life. But he has always had the will to thrive, not just survive. John can do all the things listed above—and much more. He does them on a regular basis as a routine part of life.

Several years ago, I had the privilege to meet John and see him do many of these things during a speech up on stage. As I sat there and watched him, I was amazed by what I saw! He sat down and popped off one of his shoes. Then he took off his sock and worked his magic. With his foot, he grabbed a can of soda, opened it and poured it into a glass for himself. He casually sipped from the glass throughout his speech. He could do so many things that seem impossible to do with your feet.

After his presentation, I went out into the hall and purchased his book, *What's Your Excuse?* Then I had an opportunity to speak with John in person. I held out my book and he took it with his foot. Very quickly, he placed it on the ground, opened it and flipped to the title page. As he held the book open with one foot, he grabbed a pen with the other and wrote a personal message for me. I was inspired!

John taught me a lesson on focus that I will never forget. If you get anything else out of this book, I hope you will get the significance of what he taught me. John says instead of worrying about what you don't have and what's wrong with you, **focus on what you do have**. Take what you were blessed with and focus on it. Simply do the very best you can with what you have. You can really surprise yourself with what you can do. That is such great advice! John is more accomplished and can do more than many people with arms will ever do. All because he chooses not to make excuses and instead focuses on what he can do.

If you have limitations, you just might be the lucky one. Facing odds and encountering struggle can force you to focus faster and more often than if everything is easy and smooth sailing. Take a good look at any limitations you have, then set them aside and focus intensely on what you do have. How far can you go with what you have? You just might surprise yourself!

LESSONS FROM SPORTS

I'm a big sports fan. I've always enjoyed playing sports but more than that, I enjoy watching the masters perform. No matter what the sport is, the pros all know how to focus. Playing baseball, they all say to keep your eye on the ball. That's simple yet accurate advice. The best batters are those who are best at focusing on that ball until it smacks the bat.

How about the racecar drivers? The best in car racing are those who can avoid the crashes and minimize moments of lost time. As drivers learn the sport, they learn how not to hit the wall. They focus on something other than the wall. The ones who look at the wall and try not to hit it are the ones who usually hit it.

The summer Olympics is another example. Have you ever seen a hurdler hit a hurdle and fall? The best hurdlers know that in order to clear all the hurdles, they can't focus on them. The hurdlers who focus on the hurdles and not hitting them increase their chances of actually hitting them.

My wrestling coach always emphasized the importance of focus. He told us to focus on winning instead of not losing. It's amazing how easy it was to get into a close match and fall into the trap of focusing on not losing. That was a sure recipe for losing.

BEING THE BEST YOU CAN BE

Perhaps the greatest college basketball coach in the history of the game was John Wooden. His teams won ten national championships and at one point had a winning streak of eighty-eight wins. He led his team to a completely undefeated season four different times.

Coach Wooden learned a valuable lesson from his father as a boy growing up on a farm. His father said, "Don't worry much about trying to be better than someone else. Learn from others, yes. But don't just try to be better than they are. You have no control over that. Instead try, and try very hard, to be the best you can be. That, you have control over." This lesson was one of the first things Coach Wooden drilled into his players' minds.

If college basketball players could achieve such success by focusing on being the best they could be, what can you do? Don't worry about being better than your competition. Instead, focus on becoming the best you can be in your field. How do you do that? You keep your eye on the goals that matter most in your life and keep taking one step after another until you reach your destination.

TIME TO FOCUS

Let's put this focus stuff to the test. Identify your most important goal, the one that would make you the most excited if you achieved it in the next twenty-four hours. Choose a period of time. It could be a week, two weeks, or a month. I recommend trying it for one full week at first. Write out your goal on a small card you can take with you everywhere you go. Write the goal and post it in multiple places you are sure to see throughout the day.

Every day for your trial period, do a few key things. When you wake up in the morning, think about the goal. During the day, think about the goal. Take that card out and look at it at every opportunity. When you get any pockets of free time, think about the goal and take as much action as you can toward fulfilling it. Do as much as you can during the day; then try to do a little more. When you go to bed, think of the goal. Focus on all possible angles of achieving that goal.

Like a laser beam, you will see the results of your intense focus cut through the obstacles that would keep you from reaching your goal. The more you focus, the more results you will get—and fast. This will bring in excitement and give you enthusiasm. You will be amazed at how much progress you'll make in just a matter of days. This can be life changing if you do it right.

Repeat this process over and over until you have accomplished the big goal or dream. Your self-confidence will soar and your ability to perform will increase, taking you toward bigger and better things. All this will be yours as you increase the focus in your life.

SUMMARY

"No steam or gas ever drives anything until it is confined. No Niagara is ever turned into light and power until it is tunneled. No life ever grows until it is focused, dedicated, disciplined."
— Harry Emerson Fosdick

Think about the above quote for a moment. Each of us is like Niagara Falls. For years and years, this tremendous supply of energy was wasted as the almost limitless supply of water crashed down to the bottom unused. Today, the massive energy of the flowing water is channeled into the production of a tremendous supply of power for use by mankind.

You are no different. Until you learn to focus regularly, you will fail to maximize your incredible potential. By using the principles of focus, you can regularly face and overcome seemingly insurmountable odds on a regular basis. It will become a repeatable and predictable part of your life.

Section Five

SUCCEED

CHAPTER 21

Place Self-Imposed Deadlines

"What it boils down to is deadlines."
— Jeff Blake

I have to agree with the above statement. There's always so much to do. Those "To Do" lists never seem to go away, even though you keep crossing things off. There's always something new to add, right?

During my high school and especially during my eight years of college, I must have had a gazillion different due dates. This report was due on Thursday. That project was due on Friday. These twenty pages had to be memorized for the test next week. My day planner was full of due dates and deadlines for countless things that had to be done. Why did everything have a deadline?

There is no way in this world I could have completed all the work required to become a dentist without all those deadlines. A deadline forces you to produce and gets you moving. It forces you to plan and work toward completing a specific task. A fast-approaching deadline can keep you moving all the way up to the last minute.

You need a sense of urgency to take the initiative, then get started and keep at it until the task is complete. Sometimes with tests or projects,

I didn't feel like the result was as good as it could have been. But the deadlines often brought good results that wouldn't have happened without me having a sense of urgency to get to work.

Has there ever been something on your "To Do" list that just stayed there day after day, week after week, and even month after month? I've experienced this more than I'd like to admit! I like to plan my day in writing the night before. Sometimes as I go through my planner, I see the same uncompleted task on my list over and over again. When that happens, it's because that task doesn't have a deadline. Without a sense of urgency or reason to complete it now, the task will always get put off until later.

Placing self-imposed deadlines is the best way I have found to achieve more than I ever thought possible. Take this book, for example. I have implemented many daily, weekly, and monthly deadlines for tasks that will result in a complete, published book. There are some days when I'm not particularly in the mood to write a word. However, knowing there's a deadline associated with each chapter, I am forced to sit down and write. Funny thing is, sometimes the best way to get quickly into the mood to work is just to force yourself to start working. This generates positive momentum you can build from as you accomplish that which you set out to do.

LESSON FROM A COLLEGE PROFESSOR

I'll never forget my college molecular biology class. I had two big fat books packed full of pages with teeny tiny print. There was a boatload of reading assignments, homework, and material to memorize for the tests. Just weeks into the class, I became completely overwhelmed by the enormous amount of information I had to get into my head. I mean, that class alone would have kept me busy if I didn't have any other class or thing to do that semester.

One day in particular, the professor gave us an assignment and tons of reading material for an upcoming test. All I could think was, "You've got to be kidding me! There's no way!" I looked around the room, and thankfully, I saw the others in the lecture hall felt the same way I did.

The professor sensed our strong displeasure and put his lecture materials down. He interrupted his lecture for a few minutes to teach us all a lesson about life in general. He said, "I know this is a lot a material to learn. I also know there isn't enough time for you learn it all. That's part of life. There is never enough time to get everything done." He explained how we have to take the deadlines we have, prioritize the many things we need to accomplish by those deadlines and then just do our best to get as much done as possible. That way, we stretch ourselves perhaps more than we thought we could.

Deadlines force us to perform and develop our creativity. With so much to do in so little time, we are often put into a time crunch that tends to bring out our best much faster than if we had all the time in the world. Any time I have a significant task to complete, I try to attach a deadline to it.

A colleague taught me this important lesson as it applies to business. He always said, "Work expands to fill the time available for it." He believed in placing time limits on himself for the many tasks he and his staff regularly faced. I had the opportunity to watch him in action for several weeks before opening my own dental office.

Today most of my deadlines are self-imposed. I've discovered that it is much easier to accomplish more and succeed more if I push myself. I can accomplish more now than I could have done just five years ago.

I'm not particularly smarter than I was then. Rather, I have become better at performing and producing personal results. The use of self-imposed deadlines on a regular basis is the key for me.

APOLLO 13

Have you ever been up against a serious time deadline? You know, the "make it or break it" kind? In your quest to beat the odds in anything, you will always have deadlines to meet. Some will be imposed on you and some will be self-imposed. I believe that as you become better at placing regular self-imposed deadlines, the better you will be able to beat the odds standing in your way of success.

You probably remember the 1995 Tom Hanks movie *Apollo 13*, based on the 1970 NASA near-tragedy. The public viewed the Apollo 13 space mission as just another routine mission. All that changed in an instant as these words reached mission control: "Houston, we have a problem." The astronauts had launched into outer space successfully. Then the problems began. A fault in the space module caused an explosion that turned the rest of the mission into a test for survival.

The Apollo 13 astronauts and the crew at mission control were in a race against time. With the odds clearly against them, they had a finite amount of time either to find a way or die. The ground crew and astronauts worked synergistically to quickly find a solution. The unexpected do-or-die deadline actually brought out the best in all involved. I think the best part of the movie occurs when a person at mission control predicts the spacecraft will not make it home—a disaster for NASA. The NASA flight leader on the ground disagrees and says, "With all due respect, sir, I believe this will be our finest hour."

You know the rest of the story. The event grabbed the national spotlight as people all over the United States—even the world—remained glued to their television sets. The attempt to avoid a fatal ending was a complete success. All the elements of survival came together because there was a deadline. The expert ground crew calculated how much time they believed they had and all efforts were put forth to meet that deadline. And meet it they did!

You can apply the Apollo 13 story to your own life. You have projects and tasks to complete, problems to solve, wealth to create and progress to make. If you put a deadline on the things you need to do, then you won't waste time. Instead you will enjoy greater leaps of progress toward fulfilling your dreams.

As If Your Life Depends On It

I love the book *The One Minute Millionaire* by Robert Allen and Mark Victor Hansen. In this unique book, they tell a story about a woman named Michelle, whose husband was tragically killed in an automobile accident, leaving her behind with her three children. Her wealthy in-laws didn't believe she could provide for the children, so they sought custody of them.

To retain custody of her children, Michelle was given a mandate and deadline to produce one million dollars within a year's time. Though this story is fictional, it beautifully demonstrates the principles of success. Michelle worked very hard for an entire year to find ways to earn the money by the deadline. We see her creativity multiply as she is forced to produce. She acts as though her family's well-being depends on it—because it does.

In the end, Michelle succeeded in beating the odds stacked against her. She did it by taking consistent and positive action and being in contact with those who could help her most. She rallied the support of her new friends, mentors and business partners to help her meet the deadline. She succeeded and earned permanent custody of her children.

If you really want to burn into your mind the power of being forced to meet a deadline, I encourage you to read *The One Minute Millionaire*. I can guarantee you won't be the same person again. After I read it, I wanted to place bigger deadlines on myself—as if my life depends on it. Because after all, it does.

SUMMARY

As I hope you see by now, having a deadline is not a hindrance, an irritation or something you "have to deal with." Rather, deadlines ultimately provide you more freedom by bringing you successful results faster. Deadlines can be real time savers if you use them early and often.

If you develop the discipline to place more deadlines on your most important tasks, you'll be amazed by the results. You'll focus more, stick with it longer, build greater momentum, and reap the rewards of accomplishment more often. One of the best by-products of meeting deadlines is the self-confidence you'll gain along the way. And in today's world, we need all the self-confidence we can get. And that includes you!

Which comes first—success or confidence? This isn't a "loaded" question, but it may go against what you might expect. I strongly believe success comes first. You succeed by doing. Your successes will come faster and more often as you meet the deadlines you've attached to your goals. As a result, your confidence will continue to spiral upward and beating the odds will become a regular occurrence.

CHAPTER 22

Create a Healthier You

"It is a duty to keep the body in good health.
Otherwise we shall not be able to keep our
minds strong and clear. "
— Buddha

Without health, we have nothing. No amount of wealth can ever compensate for bad health. What good is success and material progress if we aren't healthy enough to enjoy the fruits of our labors?

Can you put a price tag on any aspect of your health? What would you do if someone offered you a million dollars for your hearing? Would you take it? What about your eyesight? Would you take two million dollars for that? Would you do away with any aspect of your good health for any sum of money?

With all the technology available in the world today, nothing compares to the human body. No computer can match the human mind, any human mind. Your billion-dollar body is a priceless piece of your life.

Let's take a moment and consider your life span. How much money would you take to cut ten years from your life? How about five years? I'm sure you agree there is tremendous value in having good health.

Some people have excellent health and some are not so fortunate. One thing we all have in common is that we can all do something to improve our health. We have the power to make it better and keep it better.

A HEALTH CARE PROVIDER'S PERSPECTIVE

Over the past nine years, I've treated thousands of patients through the practice of dentistry. When I get a new patient, the first thing I do is review the patient's medical history. Routinely, I see all kinds of patterns.

People who are overweight are more likely to be taking medications for various conditions. High blood pressure, among other things, is common in this group. Some medications create a "need" for other prescription medications. As a rule, the more medications a person takes, the more problems there are to deal with. I feel bad for some of these people. Their health appears to be in a downward spiral with no seeming end in sight.

Though I don't condemn the use of prescription medications, I do believe it's best to keep them to a minimum. These medications often have harmful side effects. One oral side effect that dentists regularly see is dry mouth. The saliva glands shut down. When this occurs, the rate of tooth decay and oral deterioration skyrockets. It becomes expensive to keep the teeth from decaying. This oral side effect is just one of many that wreak havoc on the human body as a result of prescription drugs.

ADDICTIONS

Smokers always have compromised health in one way or another. Most smokers I treat would love to quit. However, their strong addiction to nicotine keeps them prisoners of its cumulative damaging effects. The harmful effects of smoking on the human body are many. Smokers tend to have a much higher incidence of gum disease, bone loss around the teeth, bad breath, strong yellow staining of teeth, lower voice, lung disease, higher incidence of cancer and more.

In addition to nicotine, many prescription pain medications, especially narcotics, are extremely addictive. Many people are addicted to these substances. The patterns, lies and stories, are very predictable. Addicts will go to almost any length to get narcotic prescriptions and refills. Lying, stealing, cheating and other destructive behaviors are routine among addicts. The sad thing is that many of these people don't believe they have a problem. For them, denial is just a river in Egypt!

How do you know if you're addicted to something? If you habitually or compulsively become dependent on something, beware. Evaluate your lifestyle to identify possible addictions you may have.

If you are addicted to anything, take a good hard look at it. Smoking, alcohol, chewing tobacco, drugs, and other addictive substances should be aggressively eliminated from your life. Get professional help and seek support from like-minded people to help you quit. Mental addictions such as pornography in any form are extremely damaging as well. Avoid pornography like the plague.

DRUGS AND YOUR HEALTH

Many TV commercials today make me cringe. Drug companies have begun to push their products directly to the public, urging them to "Ask your doctor if such-and-such drug is right for you." This is all wrong! Doctors, not patients, are trained to diagnose. It's the doctor's job to tell us what—if any—medications we need. It's certainly not up to drug companies to tell us we need to take *their* medications. Doctors don't need us to suggest which drug they may want to prescribe for us. The commercialism of prescription drugs puts undue pressure on the public to become more dependent on them.

From what I've seen, healthy people have certain traits in common. They tend to take fewer to no drugs. They lead more active lives that include regular exercise. They get plenty of rest. They eat lots of fruits and vegetables and drink lots of water. Junk food and soda consumption are kept to a minimum. They are optimistic and actively feed their minds with uplifting material. They often have a strong faith or belief in a divine power.

A HEAVYWEIGHT WORLD CHAMPION

Recently I had the opportunity to meet and hear from the three-time heavyweight Ultimate Fighting Championship (UFC) champion Randy Couture. While I'm not a fan of ultimate fighting and don't watch it, I know enough about the sport to comment on it. The sport is a mixed martial arts event, where fighters use different styles to fight each other. The UFC is now heavily regulated, but was known for being "no holds barred" when the sport first began.

In 1997, Randy Couture made his debut in the UFC Championship at the age of thirty-three. Since then, he has taken the title multiple times in both the heavyweight and lighter heavyweight divisions.

After leaving the sport for a time, at age forty-four he had an itch to step back in the octagon and go for the title again. Randy defied the odds for his age and took the heavyweight championship again. Some people have called him a modern day Rocky Balboa.

Though I am not a big fan of sports that involve fighting, I'm always interested in learning from the champions in any sport. I find that people who rise to the top of any sport or field tend to follow the same success principles.

I had the opportunity to hear Randy speak and have my picture taken with him. For the picture, I put my arm around his shoulder and raised my fist up to his chin for fun. I was absolutely blown away by how solid he is. The guy is a rock!

Randy shared some insightful advice with those of us listening to him speak. He shared some tips for getting into peak physical condition and staying there. He said to eat lots of raw foods such as oats, fruits, vegetables and food in the non-processed form. Anything with a wrapper is generally something to avoid.

Randy showed his human side as he talked about the 80/20 rule as it applies to his diet. He likes junk foods and processed food, too, and says they have their place. I love potato chips and other junk food, so it was refreshing to hear his rule of thumb. He said we should eat raw food in its natural form eighty percent of the time. Then we can use the other twenty percent of the time to toss in some junk food, if we're so inclined. If the majority of what we eat is the good stuff, then we can enjoy moments with ice cream, potato chips and all that junk!

Exercise! It goes without saying. Nothing replaces good old-fashioned exercise. Regular physical activity, especially aerobic activity, does wonders for our bodies and health. We should all be on some sort of exercise program. I want to emphasize that you should consult with your physician before you begin an exercise program. You certainly want to do what will have the best effects on your current health. Good exercise on a consistent basis will go a long way toward achieving and maintaining good health.

A GENETIC FAT MAN

Several years ago, I had an experience that changed my life. It was time to review my insurance policies, and I determined it was time to buy more coverage. The underwriters came out and did their blood pressure tests, EKG's, blood tests and so forth.

Several weeks later, the results came in the mail. As I reviewed them, I couldn't believe what I saw. My cholesterol levels were very high. I was shocked! I'm not the slightest bit overweight, and I'm a fairly active guy. I thought I ate a good diet, too. I looked at those numbers multiple times in disbelief.

It was time to visit the doctor to get some help in interpreting the numbers. My physician did a physical exam, looked at the insurance company's report and shook his head. He made me feel like a "genetic fat man," and said I needed to go on a diet. He also suggested a prescription medication to help lower my cholesterol. It was 246 and I needed to get it under 200 just to be on the high end of normal!

The moment he suggested a prescription, all I could think of were all the patients I'd seen over the years who were on prescriptions. It seems to start with just one prescription, then before you know it, there are two, three, four, five—or more—different drugs to take. I told my doctor, "No way! I don't want to go there. Isn't there something else I can do to lower my cholesterol instead of taking a drug?" He chuckled and gave me a list of things to do. I got the impression he thought it wasn't possible to lower it naturally, but he was going to let me find out on my own.

For the next six months, I did everything I could to lower my cholesterol. I routinely ate oatmeal, Cheerios, bananas and juice for breakfast. I took a multivitamin and natural garlic supplement about five times a week. I got out early in the morning before work to run eight to ten miles per week. I cut down on potato chips, fried food, junk food and seafood (even though I love shrimp. Dang!). My goal was to eat more raw unprocessed fruits, vegetables, grains and whole foods.

Six months went by quickly and then it was time to have my cholesterol checked again. I made it fun by having my staff members guess how far they thought I'd lowered my count. When the results came back, I felt like shouting, "YES!" I had lowered my total cholesterol to 196. That's a twenty percent reduction in just six months! I felt like those people on the Cheerios commercials who get excited and tell complete strangers, "Guess what? I lowered my cholesterol!"

MENTAL HEALTH IS EQUALLY IMPORTANT

"More gold has been mined from the thoughts of men than has ever been taken from the earth." — Napoleon Hill

It's not enough to keep our bodies in good physical shape. We must take care of our mental health as well. How do we do that? We must constantly feed our minds with uplifting and inspiring material. Listen to good music, instructional recordings on self-improvement, education, motivation and inspiration.

As the old saying goes, garbage in equals garbage out. Motivational speaker James Malinchak disagrees. "No! They lied when they said that," he says. "Garbage in, garbage stays. Garbage rots, garbage stinks! Garbage grows, then garbage out!" It's true. Protect what goes into your mind.

The roots create the fruits. Seeds of all kinds are planted into the fertile soil of your mind. If you don't actively pursue and plant good seeds, then the weed seeds will take over by default. It takes consistent active effort to keep the weeds of your mind cleared away so you can nourish the good seeds, which will become the positives in your life.

As we've discussed, there are key points during the day to fill your mind with the good stuff—the last twenty minutes before you go to sleep and the first twenty minutes after you wake up. That's when you want your conscious and subconscious mind to be at work on your behalf.

SPIRITUAL HEALTH

Your spiritual health is just as important as your physical and mental health. Having faith in a Higher Power or Divinity can be extremely powerful to your state of being. Determine what good spiritual health means for you and plug into the resources that help you in this area.

I've found that studying the Bible and other religious material helps me keep the right perspective on life. Spiritually uplifting music also works wonders. Being actively involved in some type of faith or Divine belief system can help you achieve and maintain a healthy balance in life.

SUMMARY

I am a big fan of the Utah Jazz basketball team. Anyone familiar with the Utah Jazz was saddened by the sudden passing of long-time Jazz owner Larry Miller. Miller owned the basketball franchise for more than twenty years. It was because of him that the team was able to stay in Salt Lake City, Utah for all those years.

Larry Miller had very strong mental health. He was an incredibly successful businessman with many automobile dealerships in the western United States. He was a brilliant entrepreneur.

As a man of faith, he had great spiritual health. He had a strong belief in God and solemn respect for what he believed to be right. He observed Sundays as a special day, a day to do only those things that brought him and his family closer to God. It was well known that he refrained from attending Jazz games on Sunday, watching them on TV or listening to them on the radio. He lived his life the best he knew so he could be at peace with himself.

At age sixty-four, Larry Miller's physical health took a nosedive as he lost his battle with diabetes. As great and as powerful as he was in business, his health deteriorated and he has passed on. His sudden passing reminded me how fragile life can be. Disease and illness respect no one.

We never know when our time will come. All we know is death will come for all of us. For some, it will come early. For others, it will come after a very long life. You can increase your chances of living longer by working today to create the healthiest possible version of yourself. Those who achieve and maintain good physical, mental and spiritual health position themselves to beat the odds over a longer period of time. Good health makes life last longer, and it's more enjoyable and more successful.

CHAPTER 23

Remember Your Successes

*"Turn your face to the sun and the
shadows fall behind you."*
— Maori Proverb

The title of this book is *Beating All Odds* for a reason. On your way to achieving your goals, you will encounter obstacles, disappointments, temporary failures, delays and unplanned challenges. It happens to everyone. It's easy to get discouraged and lose the motivation you started out with. That's why the majority of people give up far too soon. Never forget what Rudy Ruettiger says: ***It's always too soon to give up.***

It's human nature to think of failure when obstacles stand in the way of progress. But you'll find it difficult to move toward your goals when you have failure in mind. That's why it's so important to remember your past successes. If you look back at your life, you'll realize you've already had many successes, some small and some big. You most likely overcame obstacles and setbacks to achieve those successes. How did you feel about those experiences?

Remembering your successes revives the positive feelings you had in the past. It builds tremendous momentum you can apply to those obstacles you may face now.

Remember, you've faced difficulty in the past. If you remember you had what it took to succeed then, you'll gain self-confidence to overcome present obstacles and achieve your current and future goals.

I know you're thinking, "But what if I've never accomplished a goal like the one I have now—will remembering past successes that are completely unrelated help me with this goal?"

Absolutely! Naturally, your current goals aren't the same as those you had in the past. However, the mere fact that you've already proven to yourself that you can set and achieve a challenging goal is enough to move you forward in taking positive action. You'll be able to throw out the word "impossible" and replace it with, "I'm possible!"

CELEBRATING YOUR SUCCESSES

Give yourself a pat on the back when you achieve something good. It can go a long way. When you succeed, celebrate! When you celebrate your successes, those wonderful feelings of achievement and motivation etch themselves into your subconscious mind. You'll be able to draw upon these memories—and feelings attached to them—in the future.

Don't be afraid to use words of praise with yourself. Self-praise might be the most powerful praise of all. There have been times in my car when I know I've given people in other vehicles a chuckle as I enthusiastically talk, even cheer, in celebration of a success.

How do you celebrate when you accomplish something big?

I remember taking the written portion of the national board exam for dentistry. There was so much to remember from the years leading up to it. I was overwhelmed. I did the best I could and took the exam. It was difficult, but I knew I'd done my best and felt good about it.

Then it was time to celebrate. As struggling college students with limited budgets, none of us ate out very often. But that night, my wife and I joined friends from dental school at a very nice restaurant. And for once, we actually read the menu from left to right instead of the other way around! I had a delicious seafood dish that made me feel like a king. It was a relief to know I'd done my best on a difficult and comprehensive exam. Celebrating with friends and my favorite food was exhilarating. The fact that I celebrated helps me remember that successful feeling in greater detail.

Celebrating works with the small successes, too. When you do something good during the day, reward yourself. Treat yourself to an ice cream cone. Take a nice bubble bath. Take a break and do something you enjoy. Enjoy a little extra time with your hobby. What's important is that you do a little something special for yourself.

As you celebrate your successes, big and small, it will be easier for you to remember and recall them. You'll feel better about yourself now and in the future when you draw upon memories of your successful moments. Then, when you get stuck or when you face an obstacle, you'll be able to summon the momentum you need to move forward toward your goals.

GETTING THROUGH THE DARK NIGHT

When I was thirteen, I went through something I'll never forget. I was in the mountains at Boy Scout camp. This popular event was organized and directed by local and state scout leaders and gave us an opportunity to work through the steps necessary to receive the Eagle Scout award. One requirement was earning a Wilderness Survival merit badge.

In our case, three leaders took forty of us into the woods (the middle of nowhere as far as we were concerned) with limited supplies to survive the night. We were allowed only the clothes we wore, a sleeping bag, rain poncho, matches, flashlight, water and some food to cook over a fire. With that, we were left to survive and hope the weather cooperated. For us, the weather proved to be far from cooperative.

I joined three other boys and we busily prepared for the night. We built a fire and did our best to cook dinner. We ate, but we didn't eat well, to say the least! Then, as evening approached, the sky turned dark and it looked like a storm was headed our way. We quickly gathered little logs and sticks to build a small shelter for four.

Before we finished, the sky opened and rain poured down. There we were—alone in the mountains with no shelter—right in the middle of an intense thunderstorm. We were scared. Panic set in as we scrambled to gather pine branches to build a makeshift roof for our little shelter. We placed our sleeping bags inside and gathered our rain ponchos. We put them across the roof in an attempt to protect ourselves from the rain.

The storm raged on and the rain poured down. Then, to make matters worse, it got cold. The plummeting temperatures, combined with our wet clothes, were a bad combination. We were miserable and afraid. Darkness set in, and all we could do was get into our small shelter, strip off our wet clothes and get into our sleeping bags, two boys per bag, to get as warm as possible.

Conditions grew worse. Despite our best efforts with the rain ponchos, bitter-cold rainwater leaked in all around us. Before one boy was able to get his wet clothes off and get into a sleeping bag, the early stages of hypothermia set in. As Boy Scouts, we knew about hypothermia and what to do in emergencies. Well, learning about it and experiencing it are completely different things. There was nothing left to do but try to apply what we'd learned.

We helped the boy who was beginning to go into hypothermia and another who was becoming extremely cold. We stripped down to our underwear and tossed any wet clothes out of the way. Frightened, we huddled together and prayed we would survive the ordeal.

Moments later, we learned our adult leaders were in over their heads. We saw their panic as they brought some other scouts to our shelter. I guess they saw we were doing better than the others, so they told us to take in more boys. We took them in, got rid of their wet clothes down to their underwear and crammed them into the driest sleeping bags, two boys per bag.

After that, all we could do was wait and hope to get through the night. I shared my bag with the boy who was going into hypothermia. It was a one-person sleeping bag, and this kid was bigger than me, so I ended up smashed against the side of the sleeping bag. But moments after he got into my bag, my body heat warmed him up and he soon contributed to our collective survival instead of remaining a victim.

Problems and challenges persisted. The rain was unrelenting and the leaks increased. Our sleeping bags became wetter by the hour. Our shelter for four held at least twice that number. One boy began to panic due to claustrophobia. We told stories to calm him down before he went into full-blown panic and to keep everyone focused on good things.

We fought fear all night. We huddled together and battled our fears and the weather minute by minute, hour by hour. The rain kept up until morning. We were all very cold and wet, but we were alive and well. Soon, confidence replaced fear as the dark night faded into morning. The rain finally stopped and the sun began to rise. We got out of our sleeping bags, dressed, packed our things and hiked back to base camp.

It was beautiful and sunny at base camp that day. And we left as changed individuals. We had survived perhaps the biggest challenge in our lives. We were blessed in that we'd made it through the night. Together, we had accomplished something bigger than ourselves. We'd helped each other make it through the challenges of the cold, wet and dark night.

As I look back on that experience, I remember the feeling of confidence in the face of adversity. If I could get through a dire situation like that, I know I can accomplish many difficult things. I know the boys I was with that night can draw on the same memories of success and confidence. One of them is my good friend Steve Edgley, who later experienced a dark night, only on a much grander scale.

SURVIVING A MASSIVE STROKE

Steve Edgley, MD, had the world in the palm of his hand. A brilliant and successful graduate of Loyola Medical School, Steve moved on to his residency in ophthalmology. He was successful in eight years of difficult study and made extremely good grades. Prior to that, he mastered the Japanese language while he was in Japan as a church service missionary. Steve was an accomplished athlete and participated in triathlons. He was a wonderful husband and father with a beautiful family.

When he was twenty-eight years old, Steve Edgley's world crashed down in one tragic moment. Steve knew the moment it happened that something was wrong, terribly wrong. He was experiencing the symptoms of a stroke—symptoms he knew well from his years in medical school. Could it really be? Yes, Steve was having a massive stroke. Somehow, he notified his wife to get him to the hospital immediately. Soon he was in a hospital bed, unable to speak and paralyzed on his right side.

As he lay there, Dr. Edgley tried with all his might to keep thinking. He knew knowledge was his most important asset. He'd spent all those years in school to acquire it and was determined to do everything he could to keep it. Although he felt disconnected from the world, he continued to run medical emergency response patterns through his mind. "I wanted to make sure I kept all the information in there," Dr. Edgley said.

As the days passed, Steve realized that his life as he'd known it would never be the same. He could not speak and he could not move. However, he remained conscious and kept thinking. He knew if he could keep his knowledge and intellect, then somehow he'd find a way to practice medicine again. He kept his mind active through it all and never lost his memory.

"When something like this happens, it's clear that you can give up and wait to die or pick yourself up," he said. "It was either A or B, nothing in between. Give up or fight. There is no middle ground."

Steve Edgley is a fighter. Giving up is not in his vocabulary. The fact he had his knowledge gave him tremendous hope. He knew it would be a matter of time before his ability to speak came back.

While still in the hospital, Steve continued to take every step in his power to make progress, regardless how small the step. The time came when he was able to write. The first thing he wrote was a note to himself about his past successes. He decided to lean on past accomplishments to give him the confidence and courage he needed to move forward in his recovery.

Steve outlined three major life successes he could lean on. They are:

- Learning Japanese will help me regain my speech.

- My persistence in medical school will help me face the intellectual and mental rigors that will be required in my recovery.

- My experience competing in triathlons will facilitate (potentiate) my physical recovery.

Steve said, "I realized these things and wrote them down while still unable to speak and being paralyzed on the right side. What I was trying to do was remember past successes and make an appraisal of my physical and mental resources and potential to succeed. I was gearing up for the fight of my life. I knew I had a choice, and in my situation there was only a potential upside from working diligently toward my recovery. I also knew it was going to be a marathon, not a sprint."

Seven years later, Dr. Steve Edgley serves as medical director of the Stroke Rehabilitation Program at the University of Utah. Most of his work is clinical, taking care of patients and residents. Dr. Edgley gives stroke victims and their families hope, encouragement, medical care and personal attention only he is qualified to provide. His patients and their families love him and appreciate having a physician who "walks the walk and talks the talk."

Today Steve leads a very successful life. In addition to his professional achievements, he speaks well and has even competed in a triathlon. And he's not done yet! I think he's just getting started with his post-stroke life. Though it's clear that he must deal with the effects of his stroke on a daily basis, Steve doesn't dwell on it. He says, "I'm just happy to be living and doing what I can do."

Dr. Edgley has beaten tremendous odds in his life. He credits much of his progress to leaning on past successes. Now he works tirelessly to help other people overcome the obstacles standing in the way of success.

SUMMARY

"In the depth of winter, I finally learned that there was in me an invincible summer." — Albert Camus

What will happen the next time you feel depressed, discouraged, inadequate or worthless? What will you do? I hope you will rekindle the flame of self-confidence and enthusiasm by focusing on your triumphant moments. You will get those positive feelings back, which will boost your confidence. You can move forward and achieve more than ever before.

You can do it! You have what is takes to beat the odds. When you face "dark nights" in life, remember your past successes. If you don't already use this success strategy, then you're in for a treat. Be prepared to enjoy this newfound source of strength that will help you not only survive, but thrive when passing through difficult times.

CHAPTER 24

Embrace a Winning Attitude

"Oh, my friend, it's not what they take away from you that counts. It's what you do with what you have left."
— Hubert Humphrey

For the past few years, there's been spirited debate among sports analysts and fans regarding the greatest college football bowl game ever played. Lou Holtz said it might have been the 2007 Fiesta Bowl between Boise State and Oklahoma. Did you see it? It was certainly the best football game I've ever seen. Our city of Boise was on a natural high for weeks following that win.

This Fiesta Bowl featured the mighty Oklahoma Sooners, who had a great winning streak and were considered by most to be superior to the underdog Boise State Broncos. As the game unfolded, Oklahoma's advantages in both size and athleticism were evident. But the Broncos came to play and remained in control for most of the game. Then, late in the fourth quarter, the tide turned. Oklahoma made a remarkable comeback to tie the score with less than two minutes to play.

Boise State took the field with one last chance to drive down the field for the winning score. On the first play, Bronco quarterback

Jared Zabransky threw an interception that Oklahoma ran back for a touchdown. Boise State fans all over the stadium shook their heads in shock and disbelief. Many people thought Zabransky had blown it and the game was over. After all, just a bit more than a minute remained for Boise State to cover nearly the length of the field against one of the nation's staunchest defenses, for a must-score touchdown to force the game into overtime.

As far as most were concerned, the game was over. But Jared Zabransky had other ideas. After having thrown that interception, he hurried back to the sidelines with a smile on his face. He knew he and his team had what it took to find a way to win. The entire team embraced his winning attitude as the offensive unit took the field. They shook off the unfortunate interception and confidently went out to execute their winning plan. In a matter of moments, Boise State ran three of the most incredible trick plays I have ever seen. They shocked Oklahoma, forced the game into overtime and won the game on the Statue of Liberty two-point conversion trick play.

In the weeks and months after the game, the buzz across the nation gave hope to the underdogs of the world. You see, Boise State could have taken the easy way out—given up and settled for a respectable showing in a hard-fought loss. But the Broncos would not be denied—and if you have the attitude of a champion, you can overcome the greatest of obstacles.

PROACTIVE VS. REACTIVE

We've discussed the concept of being proactive instead of reactive. Stephen R. Covey masterfully teaches this and does so beautifully in his classic book *The 7 Habits of Highly Effective People*. I highly recommend this book.

We all face unpleasant and downright disappointing experiences in life. It is also true that we face the same choice each time these situations arise. We can choose to be reactive and negative or proactive and positive.

Being reactive is destructive and negative. Becoming and staying angry, seeking revenge, harboring ill feelings toward people, and wallowing in self-pity are all progress killers. Hans Selye teaches that revenge is the most destructive of human emotions. When we react to situations, we give away our power and forfeit our opportunity to grow. Nothing good comes from being reactive, so that's all I want to say about it.

Being proactive is positive. We respond to negative events by doing that which will bring about the best possible outcome. This is when our greatest successes and progress come. Everybody gets knocked down in the game of life, but only those who respond get back up. To be proactive, you must embrace a winning attitude and stand firm when disappointment strikes. If you can control your attitude, you can succeed in any endeavor you choose.

ATTITUDE

I came across this little essay several years ago and thought I'd share it with you. It sums up the importance of approaching life with a positive attitude.

Etch those words into your heart. Never underestimate the power of a good attitude! You'll be surprised at how well things go for you as

> ### ATTITUDE
> ### BY CHARLES SWINDOLL
>
> The longer I live, the more I realize the impact of attitude on life. Attitude, to me, is more important than facts. It is more important than the past, than education, than money, than circumstances, than failures, than successes, than what other people think or say or do. It is more important than appearance, giftedness or skill. It will make or break a company...a church...a home. The remarkable thing is we have a choice every day regarding the attitude we will embrace for that day. We cannot change our past... we cannot change the fact that people will act in a certain way. We cannot change the inevitable. The only thing we can do is play on the one string we have, and that is our attitude. I am convinced that life is 10 percent what happens to me and 90 percent how I react to it. And so it is with you...we are in charge of our attitudes.

you learn to control your own attitude. With a winning attitude, you can control your own destiny. Each day when you're blessed to wake up with your feet on the right side of the ground, you have a choice. Attitude is a choice. Empower yourself and make it a good one.

THE "I CAN" PROGRAM

"Motivation is the fuel necessary to keep the human engine running."
— Zig Ziglar

Recently, I attended a regular meeting of about twenty local business owners, investors and entrepreneurs. The group meets weekly to network and view motivating and educational material that empowers those in attendance to improve their businesses. That day, we watched a video presentation by Les Brown. It was exciting and inspiring to hear from an expert in success as he shared his insights and secrets.

An open discussion followed. One man's comment struck a chord with everyone in the room. He said he appreciated our meetings because they provided access to positive and uplifting information that built confidence, motivated, inspired and empowered him to succeed. Then he said, "Why don't they teach this stuff in our schools?" Everyone agreed. Wouldn't it be great if everyone had an opportunity to learn the principles of success at an early age rather than later in life?

I raised my hand to share some good news with the group. I said, "These concepts are being taught—in schools all over the country. And the curriculum is finally making its way to Idaho." Well, you could have heard a pin drop. They were all ears. Then I asked, "Have you heard of Zig Ziglar?" The reply was a unanimous and enthusiastic yes. I shared my relationship with the Zig Ziglar Corporation that goes back to 2005.

In 2005, after learning that Zig Ziglar is America's mentor, I immersed myself in his material and loved it. My professional life soared. I became a better father, husband, neighbor, friend and positive contributor to society. Many people asked me to share my "secret" to success. Through studying Ziglar and others' materials, I learned there is no "secret." The principles of success are universal and will work for everyone. They're especially effective with children.

As I learned more about Zig Ziglar, I heard of a children's program Ziglar designed more than thirty years ago—the "I CAN" program. Without a doubt, the I CAN program creates positive, measurable results in grade school students. An enormous amount of data shows kids do much better when they participate in the I CAN program, as opposed to kids who aren't fortunate enough to benefit from it. There's a sharp increase in test scores, self-confidence, respect for superiors, self and peers, along with performance during and after the school years.

In 2006, I attended Ziglar's signature event, "The Born To Win" seminar. Bob Alexander joined Ziglar as a keynote speaker for this prestigious event. Bob is an educator with incredible experience in the public school system. By then, Ziglar had turned the I CAN program over to Bob's excellent leadership. I met Bob and invested in the program. We talked about how I could bring the program to Idaho and introduce it in my kids' school. As you know, I am passionate about making my community the best it can be, starting with my own family.

It didn't work that way. The principal of my kids' school demonstrated to me that many people resist change—especially if it's not their idea. She liked the materials, but never took action to put them in place. Then last year, I took the I CAN curriculum to an elementary school my children once attended. That principal was blown away! He gladly accepted my offer to review and implement the program. Then he thanked me for being an involved parent who cared about making an impact on our children's lives. Recently, he left me an exciting voicemail to say how much the school is benefiting from the I CAN program.

Let's get back to my local networking group. As we talked about the I CAN program, the excitement and widespread interest in the room was contagious. The group rallied to support this opportunity to implement the I CAN program in our schools. One group member actually went out that very day and met with another school principal to tell him the good news. He has a local radio program and couldn't wait to talk about the I CAN program and how it helps children embrace a winning attitude at an early age.

You can learn more about the I CAN program by visiting Bob Alexander's web site, the Alexander Resource Group, at www.yesican.net.

AN ATTITUDE OF GRATITUDE

I wanted to save the best for the last. The best way I know to achieve and maintain a winning attitude is through gratitude. I never realized before what a powerful impact gratitude can have on our lives.

Over time, I learned this about gratitude: *The more you feel and express gratitude for what you have, the more you'll have to express and feel gratitude for.* Read that sentence again and again until you've memorized it. I hope you will embrace this principle.

The reverse is also true. The more we gripe and complain about what we don't have, the more we will have to gripe and complain about. Our level of gratitude, or the lack thereof, will consistently be the key to what we attract into our lives, good or bad.

Gratitude works as a powerful magnet to attract good things into our lives. A few years ago, Leigh Brinkerhoff, one of my mentors, challenged me to try an experiment. I invite you to take the challenge, too. He told me to list, on paper, everything I was grateful for. *Everything*. He said I should review the list regularly—I was in for a pleasant experience. When someone as successful as Leigh tells me to do something, I'm quick to give it a try.

And so that very day, I took a sheet of paper and started to write every good thing that came to mind and made me feel grateful. As I wrote one thing, I'd thought of another. The more I wrote, the better I felt. In the end, my list was very long! The amazing thing about this ongoing exercise is the more I review and focus on my list, the more I find to add to it.

I try to review my gratitude list regularly, especially right before bed. The problems, challenges and worries of the day seem to melt away as I focus and feel gratitude for what I have. What happens every time I do this is truly amazing. New opportunities and fortunate circumstances come my way. I feel happier and more excited about my life. I'm blown away every time I look at my list and think about everything I have to be grateful for. This is the best way I know to feel good fast and improve any circumstances.

Here's something else I discovered. Choose some part of your life that's giving you trouble. Perhaps you're facing a health challenge. Maybe you're stressed financially. It could be that you dislike your job or the people you work with. Whatever it is, take that aspect of your life and focus on everything about it that makes you feel grateful. Think of the positives and you'll find yourself feeling grateful about it pretty quickly. Then the coolest thing happens! Your circumstances will improve rather quickly. The more improvement you see, the more grateful you'll feel. This pattern continues to spiral upward as you maintain a true feeling of gratitude.

Would you like to improve or grow in a certain area of life? Besides feeling grateful for what you already have, you can take it a step further. Start feeling grateful for things you desire, but don't yet have. Think and act as if what you desire is already yours. Visualize the good things, people or circumstances you desire and be grateful for them now.

Speak it in your mind and out loud. You can use this sentence. Just fill in the blank: "I am so happy and grateful now that _____." This really works! It will get you on a frequency of receiving much faster. You'll be amazed to see how quickly this attitude attracts good things, people and circumstances into your life.

A word of warning: If you can't—or won't—feel and express gratitude for what you have, then you certainly won't be blessed with more. In fact, if you take things for granted and complain about what you have, then you're setting yourself up for failure. What you have may be taken away. Please take my word on this. I want you to be successful, happy and experience true personal growth. Being ungrateful will hinder your progress more than anything I know.

SUMMARY

Beating the odds starts and ends with one thing: your attitude. Your winning attitude will set you up for success faster and better than anything else. It's essential to focus on why you will succeed instead of why you won't succeed. One of the biggest factors in your success is the freedom you enjoy as a human being. Your attitude is perhaps the most important choice of all.

I'm going to conclude this chapter with a thought by a young girl who had every reason to be frightened, negative, angry and pessimistic. You probably already know the story of Anne Frank and the persecution her family endured at the hands of Adolf Hitler's Nazi regime. Her family was forced into hiding under the most difficult of circumstances until finally their lives were taken.

Little Anne had it all figured out. She held onto her positive attitude, despite the circumstances. Thankfully, most of us will never be forced to go through what Anne Frank endured. Living day to day in hiding, poverty and starvation, Anne stood strong. May her attitude be a reminder to us that ultimately, we are responsible for the attitudes we embrace, good or bad.

"I don't think of all the misery but the beauty that still remains."
— Anne Frank, *The Diary of a Young Girl*

CHAPTER 25

Select Your Friends Wisely

*"A man's friendships are one of the
best measures of his worth."*
— Charles Darwin

We're all familiar with the adage, "Birds of a feather flock together." This proverb speaks volumes of truth. We tend to seek out and associate with people who are like we are. I've seen this many times with people who come to my dental office.

Word of mouth advertising is the best way to build any business. We're thrilled when our favorite patients refer their friends and family. Why? Because it's almost a sure thing for us—we know the people they refer will be just like the great clients who referred them. Then our list of ideal clients gets bigger.

The flipside is also true. Clients who don't respect our time or value our services tend to refer people who are the same way. When I first started my dental practice, I took my staff to a seminar led by a great dental consultant. She warned us to avoid referrals from patients who create problems and are difficult to please. It was sound advice and a real eye-opener into the "birds of a feather" theory.

Think for a moment about the five people you associate with most. What are their personalities and professions? What about their income and careers? Are they optimists, pessimists or possibly just passive toward life? You can learn a lot about yourself by looking at the people closest to you.

Studies reveal telling patterns about one's earning potential by looking at the five people a person associates with most. For example, researchers say your income tends to reflect the average income of these five people. So if your best friends are bankrupt and unemployed, then there's a good chance you'll end up there, too. What if your five best friends are millionaires? If so, then your chance of becoming a millionaire is very good.

Here's an interesting tidbit: The wealthiest person in the U.S. associates most with the second-wealthiest person in the U.S. Why do Warren Buffet and Bill Gates associate with each other? Birds of a feather, remember? Each chooses to associate with people who are as success-minded as he is.

MASTERMIND GROUPS

The most successful and wealthiest people in the world share a secret most of us don't know. This principle is key to increasing your productivity beyond what you ever dreamed possible. Without it, you'll miss countless opportunities, untold wealth and you may never reach your true potential. But don't worry because I'm going to let you in on the secret.

Have you ever set a goal, only to realize you didn't know how to get started? Have you wished there was someone you could turn to for direction, help and advice in starting or reaching your goal? If you answered yes, then you'll benefit from this major key to success. Here's the secret: You need to become a member of a mastermind group.

A mastermind group is a collection of people who will support you in obtaining your objectives. A typical mastermind group has about five members, with a variety of backgrounds. Your mastermind group will become your support team and you in turn support others in the group as they work toward their goals. Your mastermind group can help you advance in the direction of your goals faster than you'd be able to do by yourself.

Let me give you an example of a mastermind group. Way back in the 1920's, there was a little-known automobile company named the Ford Motor Company. Its owner, Henry Ford, wanted the company to be the first to mass-produce the automobile. However, Ford did not have the capital necessary to build a plant that could mass-produce the product.

Fortunately, Henry Ford belonged to a mastermind group. He approached his group with his problem. Ford's group included Harvey Firestone (Firestone Tires) and Thomas Edison. As the group discussed Ford's problem, Firestone came up with an idea that resulted in the Ford Motor Company we know today.

Firestone proposed a plan that allowed Ford to raise the capital needed to build a manufacturing plant suited to mass production. They could pre-sell automobiles and collect in advance of the sale. Ford took this idea and pre-sold approximately 375,000 automobiles at $600 each. As a result, Ford raised $225 million through advance sales and used the money to develop the plant necessary to build the automobiles already sold.

If left to himself, Henry Ford wouldn't have been able to lead a company to become the giant in the automobile industry it is today. His success multiplied many times more than if he'd been on his own. Why? Because Henry Ford belonged to a mastermind group and benefited from the synergy of great minds coming together. No doubt Firestone and Edison also benefited from Ford's contributions along the way.

NOBODY LIKES A COMPLAINER

My Grandma Clark was famous for her great attitude. In her later years she suffered much with her deteriorating health. However, when anyone asked how she was doing, she always said, "Can't complain! You know why, don't you? Nobody likes a complainer!" She repeated the same statement nearly every time I saw her.

Grandma Clark knew a lady who always had a tale of woe to tell. She always found something to complain about. For this woman, nothing was ever good enough. My grandmother winced when she talked about this woman. Obviously, she wasn't a ray of sunshine in Grandma's life. In fact, she tried to stay away from her pessimistic friend as much as possible.

Are any of the five people you associate with most complainers? If not, that's great news for you. If so, then it's time for a cold hard look at yourself. As we've discussed, complaining will just bring more negativity into your life. Take action today to stop complaining and associating with complainers. Direct your energy to better and more productive use. You'll attract positive people to join you in a mastermind group. And as you know, the better the people in your group, the better you will become.

SNIOPS

"I will never attend an anti-war rally.
If you have a peace rally, invite me."
— Mother Teresa

Mother Teresa understood the effects of hanging around with negative people. Like attracts like. I love her quote above. If we associate with positive-minded people, it is much easier for us to remain positive. We don't have to waste energy fighting off the effects of negative people.

If you are a negative person, you must stop. Quit hanging around negative people. Zig Ziglar coined the term SNIOP, which is an acronym for Susceptible to the Negative Influence of Other People. The easiest way to decrease your susceptibility to negative people is to eliminate them from your presence. If you can't remove them from your world, then decide in advance that you won't become influenced by their negativity. Identify the people who fall into the SNIOP category and minimize your contact with them. Though they may continuously invite you to join their pity party, you can politely decline until you never get invited again. When you withhold sympathy from negative people, they soon learn you aren't the one to hear their complaints and take their complaints elsewhere.

There are two keys to dealing with negative people. First, don't be a negative person yourself. Second, do not become influenced by their negative actions. By being an optimist and avoiding SNIOPS, you will better position yourself to form a mastermind group of people just like you and enjoy the tremendous benefits that come with it.

In his classic book, *Rich Dad, Poor Dad*, Richard Kiyosaki teaches the importance of creating a group of advisors. This is another way of creating a mastermind group. You need to have a group you can work with on a regular basis to help you become better than you'd be if left alone. In business, Kiyosaki teaches the importance of hiring a good accountant, attorney and other consultants. He says to choose your advisors and then don't hesitate to pay them well. If your consultants' expert advice is making money for you, then it should be a pleasure to compensate them for it, especially if they are paid on results.

In your quest for success, it's a guarantee that you'll get there faster if you have a top-notch mastermind group. Kiyosaki says, "If I'm the smartest one on my team, I'm in trouble." Try to associate only with people who can elevate you to a higher plane.

Notice what happens as you form a mastermind group. The person you perceive as being on a higher plane than you may in turn view you in the same way. The result is a group of like-minded people who meet and work together toward the success of everyone in the group. Everybody wins.

SUMMARY

I hope this chapter has given you some new ideas to think about. The friendships and relationships you create and maintain play a huge role in how well you progress toward your goals. This applies, not only with real-life relationships, but also with the people you choose to be in contact with, be it live, via radio, television, CD, DVD, as friends or co-workers.

Associating with negative people will impede your progress and limit your happiness.

Surrounding yourself with mediocrity will likewise bring mediocre results. You will not be pushed to reach your potential.

Associating with greatness will result in greatness. It will rub off on you, and you'll be delighted to recognize it. Moving forward, it's time to select your friends wisely. It pays bigger dividends, and you'll have more fun along the way.

SECTION SIX

EXCEED

CHAPTER 26

Decide To Be Happy Today

"Let us relish life as we live it, find joy in the journey and share our love with friends and family."
— Thomas S. Monson

Everyone wants to be happy. After all, everything we strive for and do is in hopes of finding ultimate happiness. Here's the good news: happiness is a choice—your choice. Nobody can make you happy or unhappy unless you allow it to happen. A person cannot steal your happiness without your permission. No circumstance or event can make or break your happiness.

Happiness isn't tied to something in the future. But you've probably seen it in others and recognize it in yourself.

"I'll be happy when I finish school."

"I'll be happy when I get a better job or when I get a raise."

"I'll be happy when I make enough money to take my dream vacation."

"I'll be happy as soon as I get out of debt."

"I'll be happy if my co-workers stop being mean to me."

"How can I be happy with a boss like her?"

"I'll be happy when I lose weight."

It's a never-ending list and the answer is always the same. No! You won't be happy in an "if" or "when."

All too often, it's easy to let important things pass you by as you look forward to those illusive, non-existent circumstances that will "make" you happy. The key is to find happiness today, right now. If you can't find happiness today, then you won't find it when you go on that dream vacation, earn a raise or get a nicer home. There's no happy in the future if you don't know how to be happy today.

The good news is everyone can be happy. No matter who you are or where you live, no matter how much money you have, or where you work, you can be happy. We'll explore what we can do to become happy, stay happy and enjoy life right now.

HAPPY IN A THIRD WORLD COUNTRY

I learned a great deal about happiness during the time I spent in Southern Mexico. I lived among the Mexican people for a few years as part of a church service mission. I was privileged to provide humanitarian service as I lived and worked with people in the great city of Puebla, Mexico.

Where I was in Mexico, the standard of living was a far cry from what I'd experienced in the U.S. Having an automobile of any kind was a rare luxury. Water had to be treated or boiled before it was safe to drink. Many of the homes were made of concrete, adobe, aluminum and even cardboard. Most of the homes were very small and dirt floors were common. The toilets almost never flushed correctly, so it was great to have a bucket nearby with access to water.

Washing machines? Forget it. Most people didn't have one. Instead, most everyone, including me, used a concrete wash-basin. We washed our clothes, one piece at a time, against a rough cement slab. We sprinkled powdered soap on the clothes and poured cups of water over them to rinse out the soap. Then we hung them on a clothesline to dry.

So many things I'd grown accustomed to in the U.S. were non-existent or in short supply in Southern Mexico. The sewer systems and community services such as trash removal were nowhere near what I was used to. The jobs and income opportunities available were a mere fraction of what we see on any given day in the classified ads in the U.S. Many of the breadwinners I knew there made in one day what a high school kid back in the U.S. could make in less than an hour.

My experience in Southern Mexico taught me a lesson I'll never forget. Though poverty was common, the people were among the happiest I know. They didn't have many of the things money can buy, but they were rich in the things money can't buy. They had each other, and they place tremendous importance on family. Their faith is strong and they love and support each other. They focus on what they have, not on what they don't. They appreciate and have gratitude for having enough to meet their basic needs.

When I first arrived in Mexico, I was determined to immerse myself in the culture, live on a very limited budget, get to know and help as many people as possible and live like a native Mexican. An amazing thing happened while I was there. I grew to love the people and experienced some of the happiest times of my life. I learned from many of the greatest people on the planet that happiness is truly a choice. And it's our choice each day of our lives.

FOCUS ON ABUNDANCE

Our current level of happiness goes hand in hand with what we choose to focus on in life.

I love the way well-known author Sarah Ban Breathnach explains this principle:

> Both abundance and lack (of abundance) exist simultaneously
> in our lives, as parallel realities. It is always our conscious choice
> which secret garden we will tend. When we choose not to
> focus on what is missing from our lives, but are grateful for the
> abundance that's present—love, health, family, friends, work, the
> joys of nature, and personal pursuits that bring us (happiness)—
> the wasteland of illusion falls away and we experience heaven on
> earth.

In the last chapter, we talked about gratitude as one of the most powerful of human emotions. So much good comes from having strong feelings of gratitude for the good things in life. The fastest way I know to become happy and stay happy is constantly to reflect on all you have and be grateful for it all.

The ancient Roman philosopher and poet Horace shared this principle of happiness. He said, "Whatever hour God has blessed you with, take it with grateful hand, nor postpone your joys from year to year, so that in whatever place you have been, you may say that you have lived happily."

Gratitude fosters happiness.

The Golden Rule

Do unto others as you would have them do unto you.

We touched upon the Golden Rule as one of Coach Lou Holtz's three rules of life. This well-known Christian teaching from the Bible is known and used in cultures throughout the world.

It doesn't cost anything to be kind. If you think about it for a moment, you can apply this rule without much effort. Give it a try. As you go about your day, search for ways to brighten someone else's day.

A simple smile can go a long way. Whether you are dealing with a customer, paying for the groceries, going to the bank or eating out, you can always smile at the people you come into contact with. How do you feel when somebody smiles at you and makes you feel important? You feel good. The other person feels good, too. If you're a manager or supervisor, your smile will go a long way with the people you lead.

Call people by their names. The most pleasant word a person can hear is his or her own name. Put some effort into remembering the names of people you deal with during the day. Customers feel more important when you pleasantly and repeatedly say their names. Add a smile and you have a winning combination. Plus, it feels good to realize someone feels important because of having dealt with you that day.

It's easy to implement the Golden Rule in your daily life. Let me share a story of a way I found to treat someone as I'd like to be treated. Back when I delivered produce to grocery stores, I saw a pattern. The grocers liked their produce to arrive early. Many of them had unrealistic expectations about how fast I could get the produce to them, though.

They'd be irritated, angry, or upset no matter how hard I worked to get there early. "Early" to me was never early enough for them.

Naturally it was easy for me to get irritated with them. You know, thoughts like, "Who is he to be mad at me? I bust my tail to get here as fast as I can and he never appreciates it. In fact, all these produce managers ever do is complain!" The more I thought about it, the more irritated I became. With thoughts like that, how could I be happy and enjoy my job? There was no way. That's why I had to do something to change how I felt about these people, even though it seemed they didn't appreciate my service.

One day I had an "Aha!" moment. I decided to try and put myself in the other guy's shoes. I thought about what I could do to make his day better, no matter what kind of mood he was in. I was not going to give him permission to put a damper on my day. I arrived at a supermarket with my truckload of produce. I walked into the cooler to a sight that is fairly typical in the industry. Boxes, partial cases of produce, disorganization and disorder were everywhere.

I clearly remember thinking, "It won't cost me anything to be kind today." I could bring in my load, rotate the product by putting the new stuff behind the old stuff, clean the cooler, quickly organize it and make it look really good. I reasoned to myself that if I moved fast, I'd get some great exercise. I could get great exercise, brighten somebody else's day and make myself happy all at the same time! This really worked. It made lots of people happy, including me. I enjoyed it so much, that I made it a part of my routine with all the stores.

One day, my boss at the produce business pulled me aside and told me how much he appreciated me. He said I had become a real asset to the business. He made it clear I could have a great future with them if I wanted it. Isn't it neat what results from using the Golden Rule in life?

DOING GOOD DEEDS

The Golden Rule includes doing good deeds for others. The more you serve others, the more you will love them and the happier you will be as a result. But, how do you do something nice for somebody who irritates you? Have you ever wondered how or why you should treat people with kindness when they do something that upsets or offends you?

One day I was traveling with my wife and five children on vacation. It was lunchtime, so we exited the freeway and found an Arby's. We pulled up to the drive-thru and ordered lunch. They seemed to be taking a long time. But, we reasoned, our order was pretty big. As I sat there, I couldn't help but notice the lady in the car behind me. She was obviously irritated at being stuck behind a minivan full of kids that was holding things up. Her unpleasant facial expressions and non-verbal communication, designed to show me how irritated she was, continued until the window finally opened. All the while, I found myself becoming a little irritated with her. "Come on lady. Just chill and relax," I thought. "It's not my fault they're taking so long." The more I thought about it, the more irritated I became. I was giving my power away, and I wasn't happy at that moment.

Then it occurred to me: I was in control and I could decide to be happy. I made a decision to treat that lady the way I'd like to be treated. I thought to myself what it would be like if I were in a hurry and was stuck behind a minivan full of kids that was taking forever. Then I thought of something I could do to help both of us feel happy at the same time. As I gave the cashier my credit card to pay for our lunch, I told her to swipe it again to pay for the order of the lady behind us. You should have seen the look on the cashier's face! This was fun. She charged my card for her order and handed me the receipt. I asked her to tell the lady to have a nice day and we drove off.

Now, I never met that lady and never saw her reaction to my act of kindness. I didn't need to. But let me tell you what I did see. In a matter of minutes, I went from being irritated to being very happy as we left the fast food parking lot and entered the busy traffic. I was changed from the inside out. I knew I had brightened someone's day and that made me happy. No doubt my small act of kindness probably brightened her day and made her happy. It probably put her in a good mood and perhaps motivated her to show kindness to someone in her world, too.

SUMMARY

You hold the key to the door of your own happiness. You can take positive and definite action on a daily basis to bring happiness into your life. Focusing on the good things in life helps you keep the right mindset to attract happiness.

Forgive people who may have wronged you and move on. It has been said that revenge is the most destructive of human emotions. A sure way to get rid of hateful feelings toward others is to forgive them and show kindness. When you show kindness to others and serve them, you learn to love them. You love whom you serve and you serve whom you love. Happiness is the result.

Gratitude fosters happiness on a grand scale. A powerful way to get happy fast and stay happy is constantly to think about all the wonderful things you have. By focusing on what you have to be grateful for, you'll have increased feelings of gratitude that will result in increased happiness.

Decide to be happy today, right now. When you do, you'll be better able to enjoy life and smell the roses along the way.

CHAPTER 27

Work To Live

"The bitterest tears shed over graves are for words left unsaid and deeds left undone."
— Harriet Beecher Stowe

LIVING TO WORK

I remember very well the first college chemistry class I ever had. Inorganic chemistry was required for all students wishing to attend dental and medical school. The class had a reputation for being difficult. The odds of getting an A were slim.

I decided I was really going to go after it. As a young single college student, I had the freedom to pour lots of time into my studies, initially at the expense of play. After a few chemistry homework assignments and tests, I realized I was in a dogfight for a good grade. The professors limited the number of A's they gave out.

I was working very hard to go after that A. Clearly, the time and attention I was putting into that class was putting me way out of balance concerning my social life and play. I was not taking the time to recharge and rejuvenate.

One weekend I had an experience I'll never forget. I was determined to study all day Saturday at the University library so I would be sure to get ahead. In fact, I had been doing that every Saturday. As I was heading up to the campus library to study, my friend Steve was heading back to his apartment. We were both in the same chemistry class. We had the same demands placed upon us with homework and a test approaching.

In that moment, Steve taught me a life lesson I still try to live today. As we passed by each other, we stopped to talk for a moment. He told me he was going back to his apartment so he could get his things together to go skiing. I thought he was nuts as I reminded him we had a test coming up. I told him I was going to do lots of studying that weekend with no play. It was in that moment that Steve paused and said, "Taylor, we work to live, not live to work." And with that he went his way and I went mine.

WORKING TO LIVE

I replayed that sentence in my mind over and over again. I still do today. From that moment, I looked at my studies a little differently. I became better at saying enough is enough and now it's time to play. I started to carve out more time for a social life and dating. That led to finding my wife Jannie and convincing her to marry me.

With that same mindset my friend gave me, Jannie and I decided not to put off starting a family until all the schooling was done. One by one the children came during those school years, and I did my very best to remember to "work to live."

As my undergraduate years came to an end, I had earned my Bachelor of Science degree. I also was accepted to a good dental school. I had heard quite a bit about the rigors of dental school. As a father and leader of a young family, I decided to approach dental school with the "work to live" mentality.

I set time limits on the amount of time I was willing to dedicate to school. I recognized there was a significant time commitment required, but I was unwilling to neglect my family for academic success. Together with my wife, I determined the maximum amount of time during the week I would set aside for school. We decided that Sundays were a day of rest and no school-work would be done at all. This day was to be spent together as a family and for church attendance.

I set limits during the week and on Saturdays. I had so many days where I would just go to school and work as hard as I could until the predetermined time came. At that point, ready for any tests, projects, homework or not, I was done. I was determined never to drift into the "live to work" terrain.

Magic things resulted from sticking to this plan. I was able to focus with a greater sense of urgency knowing there were limits on my time. The tests would come and go and so would the seemingly endless projects. The grades always turned out just fine. Did I get a 4.0 in dental school? No, and I'm okay with that. However, I did well and gained confidence in my knowledge and clinical abilities.

I honestly look back on those crazy busy dental school years with fondness. By limiting my working time and doing my best with the time I had, we were able to build many strong family memories that will last forever. Those were some happy times.

ELIMINATE THE DEATHBED REGRETS

You will never see a tombstone that says, "I wish I had spent more time at the office." All too often it's easy to lose the balance in life. In our quest to prosper financially and succeed in the workplace, there's often a tendency to neglect the most important things.

One hundred years from now, what is going to be of lasting importance? The issues with work and career activities will likely be distant memories. If we sacrifice our family relationships, friendships, and those things that matter most at the expense of work, we really aren't experiencing true and lasting success. How we enjoyed life together with our loved ones along with our positive contributions to humanity are going to be of lasting importance.

If we put all our focus on our work all the time, our family relationships will suffer. We will not be able to be the father, mother, brother, sister, son, daughter, or friend we should be. Nobody wants to have a life of regret full of precious moments that are forever lost. Make every day count!

To Parents

"Many of us spend many years learning how to earn money in a job or business. We spend countless hours poring over books, attending lectures, studying facts and developing skills to be able to give value to the world in the form of some vocation. Conversely we spend very, very little time learning how to be parents, our most important job."
— Dr. James G. Drake

Parents need to be careful not to fall into the trap of thinking life will be better when the kids are grown and gone when they won't be so busy. Decide today to live in the moment with your children and loved ones. Longing for an easier future without the activity packed days that come with little ones can easily rob parents of some of life's greatest treasures. Building memories with your children gives you something you can keep forever, long after they are grown and gone.

I love the counsel that Thomas S. Monson recently gave to parents of young children. He said:

If you are still in the process of raising children, be aware that the tiny fingerprints that show up on almost every newly cleaned surface, the toys scattered about the house, the piles and piles of laundry to be tackled will disappear all too soon and that you will—to your surprise—miss them profoundly.

When was the last time you hugged your child for no good reason?

Regarding Friends and Loved Ones

The enemy named regret can easily creep into the life that's out of balance. In today's fast-paced society of "gotta go, gotta run, hit it hard and get it done," we can lose focus on our most important relationships. It's all too easy to take others for granted, until the day comes when they are gone from our lives. Nobody wants to be left with feelings of "if only" or "what if."

Never let something on the "To Do" list become more important than a person to be loved. Give your parents, children, or spouse a hug more often. Take the time to say, "I love you" more. Invest time in those who are most important to you. Working together, serving together, and having fun wholesome recreational activities will create lasting memories. Relationships will be strengthened.

Summary

In 1998 there was a movie created that shows the "real" story of Cinderella. It's called *Ever After*, starring Drew Barrymore. This classic movie is one of my wife's favorites.

You know the Cinderella story. Cinderella and the prince fall in love with each other. They pass through many obstacles until they are finally united in marriage. At the end of this version of the story, the narrating voice arrives at the point where you'd typically expect to hear, "And they lived happily ever after." But those were not the ending words in this movie. Instead the narrator said that the important thing is "They lived."

By determining who and what is most important in your life, you can be sure to keep a proper balance. Remember what it's all about. Working to live, rather than living to work, will help you beat the odds in your life without having any regrets.

CHAPTER 28

Give Back

*"Tithing always gives the greatest return
on your investment."*
— Sir John Marks Templeton,
Philanthropist and Entrepreneur

Through years of studying the lives of extremely wealthy people, I've found a common thread unites them all. They understand the same laws and principles of wealth accumulation. They know and use the laws of money. In almost every case, they give back.

In one way or another, these wealthy people participate in some form of tithing. In other words, they donate the first ten percent (or more) of their incomes to charities or churches in their communities. They do this regardless of their religious affiliations. They understand that sharing means having more. They believe one cannot give a crust without receiving a loaf in return.

Giving multiplies prosperity many times over. So no matter how much money you have, giving from the heart puts you in an abundance consciousness rather than giving you a poverty mindset. Givers with an abundance consciousness understand that giving actually expands money and resources rather than depleting them.

If you study the lives of most wealthy people, you'll see that the more they gave, the more they received. Is this purely coincidence? I say not. Almost every spiritual path teaches about the abundant universe and how it relates to giving. My favorite passage regarding this principle is found in the Bible:

> *"Bring ye all the tithes into the storehouse, that there may*
> *be meat in mine house, and prove me now herewith,*
> *saith the Lord of Hosts, if I will not open you the windows*
> *of heaven, and pour you out a blessing, that there shall not*
> *be room enough to receive it."*
> — Malachi 3:10

According to a Gallup Poll estimate, ninety-five percent of North Americans believe in God. In the passage above, God promises blessings in abundance to those who are willing to give. This promise works for everyone, regardless of religious beliefs. Some say the universe gives back in abundance. However you choose to see it, giving is the highest form of manifesting your true nature. It's just like a boomerang. When you give of your time, talents, money and abundance, your prosperity is multiplied coming back to you.

Those blessed to have wealth in great abundance are in a great position to give. Wealthy people dot the globe as some of the world's greatest philanthropists. However, giving is not an act reserved for the wealthy. Everyone can give, especially in moments when we feel we have nothing to give.

Millionaire Boot Camp

Recently, I attended a business marketing event led by Jay Geier, a successful business consultant. His clients do very well and prosper financially as they provide greater value to the marketplace.

Jay invited me to be a guest presenter and talk about my dental assisting school opportunity at his "Millionaire Boot Camp." I stayed for the entire event and listened to him speak and teach over the two days. Though my reason for going to the event was to share my business with Jay's dentist clients, I benefited from Jay's wisdom as he explained the principle of giving. Jay is a no-nonsense guy who doesn't hold back. He tells things the way he sees them.

Jay taught us about the importance of giving money away. I don't know anything about his religious affiliation. And that's not important in sharing his message. We heard from a rather ambitious, aggressive, honest and successful businessman who told us to decide now to give some money away. He taught us how to become wealthy using the same strategies he does.

For the umpteenth time, I found myself learning the importance of giving back from a very affluent business man. Of all the things he could have talked about in his "Millionaire Boot Camp," he chose to talk about giving first. Jay didn't just skimp over the subject and say giving might be a good thing to do. He spent a great amount of time teaching his philosophy of giving.

Jay's philosophy is similar to that of almost every wealthy person I've met or studied. He told us to plan to give some money away. And not later. Not when it's more convenient, not when we make more money, but right now. It's the philosophy I've heard so many times: giving from the heart puts you in an abundance consciousness, which puts you in a greater position to receive.

Here's what two bestselling authors said about this principle in their book *The One Minute Millionaire*:

> *"Just like water expands when it's heated, money expands when it is given away. Giving literally magnifies, multiplies and*

exponentializes money. Conversely, the tighter you squeeze
your money, the more compact it becomes....Tithing is a money multiplier,
not a money subtracter."
— Robert G. Allen and Mark Victor Hansen

BE A GENEROUS GIVER

"Giving. It's the right thing to do and it just feels good."
— Dr. Taylor Clark

Have you wanted to give back, but felt like you just couldn't do it then? Perhaps you felt the need to wait until you had more money, time or resources before giving some of it away. Something happens to you inside and out, no matter when you decide to give.

In 2008, I learned of an African man who made his way to the United States many years ago. He battled tremendous odds as he escaped poverty in his own country. He came here with the vision of learning how to generate interest and funds to bring the right people together and build a school for the impoverished children in his village back in Africa.

His mission and vision came to my attention during a series of down weeks in my dental business. I wanted to donate to his cause and knew it would be a good thing to do. However, cash flow was very tight and I didn't want to borrow funds from my other businesses. I knew it was a difficult moment to give. Nevertheless, I'd seen many times in my life that giving multiplies prosperity.

I decided to share this principle with my dental staff. They knew we were struggling with cash flow during this particular month. They knew the economy was in a deep recession. I sensed their worry about keeping their jobs. I knew how tight things were. We sat down and looked at our rather empty schedule for the day. Business hadn't been very good in the few weeks leading up to that, and it wasn't looking very good in the days after either. This reminded them I was well aware we were having a tough time. I told them about the school in Africa and the children's needs. I said their problems were far worse than ours and they needed our help. I shared with them my belief that you can't give from the heart without receiving abundance in return in some form or another.

Then I asked my secretary to get the company checkbook and print a check for $1,000 for the school in Africa. I said, "We are going to give. Take a good look at the schedule and remember how things are right now. You'll be amazed at what happens in the next two weeks as a result of our giving. Sometimes the best time to give of ourselves is when we don't think we can." I emphasized that in addition to giving, we would continue to do all we could to take positive action toward improving our situation.

In a matter of two hours, an existing patient came in needing approximately $3,000 in dental work. She hadn't been able to afford it when I first diagnosed it, but she had come up with the funds to get it done, and she wanted it done right away! Coincidence? I don't think so. We did the work and she was grateful we'd been able to accommodate her right away. We were paid well *and* ended up being her heroes! In addition, several new patients called and scheduled appointments; one wanted an evaluation for a large cosmetic dentistry procedure.

Needless to say, my staff was blown away. At mid-day, my assistant said, "Dr. Clark! You told us to watch what happens over the next two weeks. It only took a few hours to see a dramatic change in our schedule!" She thought it was very cool and so did I. It didn't surprise me, but I was very grateful for our sudden change in productivity.

Giving is the right thing to do.

GIVING VS. RECEIVING

We all have something to give away. Giving doesn't have to involve money. In fact, some of the greatest gifts we can give don't have anything to do with money. Giving of our time, expertise, resources and attention can go a long way with those in need. There will always be a need for us to give. When we exercise our giving muscle, it gets stronger and our ability to make a positive impact on the world increases. How does it feel to give? I think most people would agree—it feels fulfilling, joyous and wonderful.

Remember, giving is but one side of the coin. You may wonder what's on the other side. The other side of the coin is receiving. Have you heard the saying, "It's better to give than to receive?" A lot of people believe this statement, but I'm going to challenge it. In fact, I completely disagree with it. Giving and receiving are on opposite sides of the same coin. For every giver, there has to be a receiver. It's logical, then, for every receiver, there has to be a giver. You can't have one without the other. The two must be in perfect balance and are equal in importance.

To become wealthy, successful, and prosperous or beat the odds in any endeavor, you have to learn to be a good receiver as well as a giver. Receiving is just as important as giving! You can't reject or turn down people, opportunities or resources that come your way as you pursue your goals. If you're not willing to receive your share of abundance, it will go to another person. Furthermore, as you reject good things that come to you, you more powerfully stop good things from coming to you in the future.

We have talked about how good and fulfilling it is to give. But what happens when you want to give and the other person rejects your gift? Most of us would agree we feel horrible when that happens. When we are unwilling to receive, we deny others the opportunity to feel good by giving. T. Harv Eker takes it a step further by saying, "If you are not willing to receive, then you are 'ripping off' those who want to give to you." Instead of them feeling joy and pleasure from giving, they feel lousy and sometimes rejected.

Eker also said, "If you aren't willing to receive your share, it will go to someone else who is. That's one of the reasons the rich get richer and the poor get poorer. Not because they're any more worthy, but because they are willing to receive while most poor people are not."

SUMMARY

Giving back is one of the most important things we can do in our quest to create wealth and build financial independence. We put into circulation much good in this world and the natural order of things dictates we will be positioned to receive as long as we don't block things from coming to us. Giving blesses the lives of others and at the same time serves as a prosperity multiplier for the giver.

I don't know how the natural laws governing the universe work. What I do know is that they work whether we understand them or not. I have tried to be a generous giver, and I've also received great and often unexpected abundance in one form or another.

Though we don't give just so we can get, we need to be aware that opportunities to receive will come. The perfect balance must exist. Before I had the understanding of this principle I now have, I'd see a penny on the ground and ignore it. "Why waste time bending over for a mere penny?" I'd think. Today I think differently. I can't tell you how many pennies I've found over the past few years. Every time I see one, I excitedly pick it up and think or say, "Thank you!" I've found the better I get at receiving, the more this world wants to give me. It's often much, much bigger than a penny!

CHAPTER 29

Finish Strong

"I never lost hope."
— Jason Lezak, 2008 U.S. Olympic Swimmer

Have you ever gotten off to a slow start with something you set out to accomplish? Perhaps the thought of falling behind caused you to lose hope and you felt like giving up. Let me tell you a story.

In 2008, the world witnessed one of the greatest comeback victories in sports history. The stage was the Olympic Games in China. In mens' swimming, the U.S. Medley relay team was up against the heavily favored French team. Many didn't think it was possible for the U.S. to beat the French.

Three of the four U.S. swimmers had finished their leg of the relay race and it was time for Jason Lezak, the oldest of the swimmers at age thirty-two, to attempt the unthinkable. After all, he was starting out significantly behind the great French swimmer Alain Bernard, who held the world record. As the two swam the first length of the pool, it appeared Bernard was extending his lead.

As they flipped against the wall and had twenty-five meters remaining, Jason Lezak was nearly a full body length behind Bernard. The NBC-TV announcers said they didn't think it was possible for Lezak to overtake Bernard. In fact, they declared the U.S. team as the silver medalists. Then the unthinkable gradually turned into reality.

With each stroke, Lezak appeared to be gaining ground on Bernard. The crowd and TV announcers went wild. As the final seconds of the race closed, the world knew Lezak was doing something incredible. He hadn't just come back—he had a chance to beat the great Frenchman to the wall.

Jason Lezak lunged for the wall and out-touched Bernard by a fingertip—eight hundredths of a second, to be exact. The world record had been shattered. It was by far Lezak's best 100 meters ever. In an Associated Press report, Lezak said, "I don't know how I was able to take it back that fast, because I've never been able to come anywhere near that for the last fifty."

How did he do it? He never lost hope. He knew he'd started out significantly behind and had much ground he needed to make up. He didn't fret about how far he had to go or how much time was left to do it. Instead, he focused on representing the United States and knew he'd do nothing short of his very best to represent his country. He kept at it, stroke by powerful stroke, until the last millisecond of the race.

As I watched that race unfold on my screen at home, I got goose bumps. I've since watched it many times over. Jason Lezak shocked the world by showing a perfect example of how to finish strong. His accomplishment gave millions of people hope. He played a huge underdog role in starting so far behind, let alone needing to catch up with the world's best swimmer in this event.

Are you behind in a race right now where you got off to a slow start? Perhaps you are behind and have to make up seemingly impossible ground in order to accomplish your objective. Like Lezak, you must not lose hope. Rather, take each moment and do the very best you can. Small actions, consistently repeated, can produce big results.

A SCHOLARSHIP OUT OF REACH

As a teenager, I always knew I wanted to attend Brigham Young University after high school. I'd attended many BYU football games during the years when the great Lavelle Edwards was coach. Being on the campus and experiencing the campus environment fueled my desire one day to be a student there.

As I've shared, I always tried my best in high school. I made good grades, but only because I worked very hard for them. I was never a straight-A student and wasn't even close to being valedictorian or anything like that. Besides that, I've always been lousy at taking standardized tests such as the ACT or SAT.

I studied hard to prepare for the ACT test. Despite my studies, I was disappointed with my score. So I did what any determined person would do. I signed up to retake that blasted ACT test. I studied longer and harder than before. The result? My second score was only slightly better than the first score. Considering how hard I'd worked, I just didn't think it was fair that a university admissions committee would place so much weight on a silly test. I knew the test wasn't an accurate method to predict my capabilities in college.

Fortunately, BYU accepted me. But an academic scholarship? No way. They only went to kids who had extremely high grade point averages and high ACT scores. I was happy to have been accepted, and I knew I had done my best.

When I began my studies at BYU, I met many academic scholarship recipients in my pre-dental science classes. From what I could tell, they had to put their pants on one leg at a time just like I did. A friend informed me that these students had to maintain a certain grade point average or they would lose their scholarships. He also told me it was possible for me to earn that scholarship when somebody else lost it.

Like many times in life, I had not started off well. Though I tried hard initially, I had been denied an academic scholarship. During my freshman year, I continued to do my best, just as I always had. I worked and studied hard in all my classes. Good grades resulted. Though I never got a 4.0 in any one semester, my grades were consistently high.

Payday finally came. Near the end of my first year of college, I received a letter from the University. I had been awarded an academic scholarship as a reward for my first year results! I was able to keep that scholarship all through the rest of my BYU years, which saved me thousands of dollars in tuition. I knew several students who received academic scholarships right out of high school, only to lose them after their first year. All I could do was smile and think about how well life pays those who finish strong.

A Pattern to Follow

In his study of the world's most successful people, Hill observed a pattern they all shared. Most of them seldom if ever got off to a good start. They all experienced discouragement and temporary failures. They passed through many trying and difficult times before they finally "arrived." Sometimes it took being brought to a moment of crisis or despair before the great ones finally met their "other selves."

It is the same for you and me. Recognize that you hold the key to your own success. If you don't quit, but just keep going, you will get there! Keep at it no matter how long it takes and no matter how many failures you encounter. Billionaire Bill Bartmann claims he has failed more times than anybody he knows. What makes him and other successful people different is that they never quit. They do their very best to finish strong.

I don't know about you, but this gives me great hope and has for many years. I can't tell you how many times I have gotten off to a bad start. I've learned how to finish strong out of necessity. Even in dental school, there were so many times when my first tests or projects had dismal results. I knew then, as I know now, it doesn't matter how badly you start because you always have a chance to finish strong. Some of my best test scores came from persistently working to overcome and absorb losses from earlier setbacks.

This same pattern applies to my businesses. Some of my best months have come after a poor start. A slow or poor start is absolutely meaningless unless we stay at that low level of accomplishment. Of course, I don't advocate starting off slow on purpose. You should always try to get off to the best start possible in everything you do. However, no matter who you are or what you do, you'll have plenty of bad starts where you will be way behind in the game of life.

When slow starts happen and setbacks occur, you have a decision to make. Will you settle for mediocrity or will you determine to find a way to speed things up? Merely recognizing a slow start and being behind in your quest to beat the odds is actually a step in the right direction. If you know that where you are now is far from where you want to be, then you can begin to take positive action at once. You can gain the ever-important momentum needed to carry you to the finish line at a much faster pace than when you started.

SUMMARY

Decide today to finish strong. Search for ways to turn seeming failures into your greatest strengths. The winners of life's races are seldom the naturally gifted, smartest or most talented people. Instead, the winners are more often ordinary people like you and me who just keep at it and determine to finish strong in everything they do.

I'd never advocate not trying for the very best grades in school. But I want to leave you with a thought that holds true in many situations. How many A students out there today work for C students? You might be surprised if you knew! This world rewards well those who finish strong.

The point I'm trying to make is that no matter who you are, how far behind you are, how untalented or unintelligent you may think you are, there is tremendous hope for you if you persistently strive to finish strong. Be relentless and persistent in your pursuit of a strong finish in everything you do. Do this and your success in life will multiply before your eyes!

CHAPTER 30

Living The Dream

"Success is the progressive realization of a worthy ideal."
— Earl Nightingale

If you are progressing toward your worthy ideal, then you're already a success. I hope you are living in a way that truly brings you closer to your dreams, whatever they may be.

Success principles will always be what they are. They have not changed in thousands of years, and they work for everyone. People who choose to follow them will soon find themselves living their dreams. They will be in complete harmony with who they are and who they wish to become.

HAVING WHAT YOU WANT VS. LOVING WHAT YOU HAVE

Living the dream starts with learning to love what you have before you yearn for more. Before wanting a better job, learn to appreciate the one you have. Before wanting more money, be grateful for the money you currently have, no matter how much. Instead of wishing your spouse was more this or more that, focus on your spouse's good qualities. Before you feel sorry for yourself for not having more, think about the abundance you already have. You may find yourself surprised by how good you already have it.

When you truly take on the right mindset and love what you have, you'll be on the fast track to having more of what you want. You'll see the world through ROSE-colored glasses instead of WOES-colored glasses. Seeing opportunities becomes easier in the midst of adversity. Appreciating what you have and graciously taking what comes brings success-building momentum. Your life will become a magnet gaining strength in attracting the good things to it.

I've already shared wisdom from a man I deeply admire, Joseph B. Wirthlin. He recently passed away. Shortly before his passing, I heard him speak. He talked about loving what you have. He shared a lesson he learned as a boy from his mother. One day his football team lost a tough game and young Joseph was very discouraged. He went home and shared his sad story with his mother. Throughout life, his mother repeated the same words she said to him in that moment. She said, "Joseph, come what may and love it."

In your pursuit of success, you will have highs and lows. Don't get too high with the highs or too low with the lows. When discouragement comes remember—the way you respond to it is key to determining how successful and happy you can be in life. If you choose to love your life, then you can be happy.

ADVICE FROM A YOUNG GUY

Early in my career as a dentist, I hired a business coach to help me build my business. I still remember a recording he sent me. He was only twenty-eight years old at the time, a few years younger than me. Fortunately, I didn't dismiss his expertise because of his age. Instead, I saw he was wise, well beyond his years.

In those days, I could call his office and sometimes he answered the phone himself. His business was in its infancy. But based on some of the sound principles of business and success he taught, I knew his business wouldn't be small for long. Today, just five years later, he's a consultant to dentists and business owners around the world. He has multiple businesses that produce millions of dollars in revenue every year in return for the value he has added to the world. All the money I've paid him has come back to me in multiples.

Years ago, I flew across the country to meet this business coach. One thing he shared really resonated with me and has stuck with me ever since. He strongly encouraged us, his clients, to build our work around our lives—not the other way around. He reminded me that it's my life and I should protect it. He said we're free to choose the type of lives we want to live rather than let work dictate the future for us.

I came away from the meeting determined to design the life I wanted to live. I'd then fit work and making a living around it. I knew too many other doctors who'd gone through years of difficult study, only to end up prisoners of a J-O-B that consumed and controlled their lives. I decided I wasn't going to let that happen to me, no matter what stood in the way. This life strategy has made all the difference in the world for both my family and me. As I conclude this book, I'm going to share my version of "living the dream" in hopes it may inspire you to strive to live yours.

A DREAM WORK SCHEDULE

As I pondered what I'd learned from my mentor about building work around my chosen lifestyle, I got excited. The thought of taking control of my schedule and choosing how I spent my time inspired me. My first priority was to be the best husband I could be for Jannie. First, I decided to end my Monday office hours at one o'clock. I could get up as early as I wanted and work as intensely as I wanted, but when one o'clock rolled around, it became Jannie's time. I was home to take over with the kids. My intent was to give her time to do whatever she wanted to do. I know I'm the one with the easier job. Being able consistently to set aside time for her to be able to play catch up or get ahead is a great feeling.

I have chosen to treat my dental patients three days per week for about six hours each day. I start early in the morning and try to finish up by one o'clock each day. I do only those aspects of dentistry that I most enjoy. If patients really want to see me, they'll come during the hours I'm there. Otherwise, my associate dentist provides excellent care and the services I choose not to do. This schedule gives me tremendous flexibility to work on my businesses and on my own education. I can actually work when it's most convenient for my family and me. Some of my most productive work is done after the kids have gone to bed, before they wake up or while they are at school.

My schedule allows me to do many things that are important to me. Just a few days ago, I volunteered in my daughter's third-grade class. A few months before that, I met with business owners from the community to rally support for improving our local public school system. I've had the opportunity to meet with the principals of my kids' schools and offer my time and financial support to improve the quality of education my children and their peers receive.

If we have an important family event such as a funeral, family reunion, wedding or any other unexpected event, we go. A full-time doctor works for me. I hire him to fill in for me when I choose to be away. I've also developed friendships with many dentists in our community. Any one of them can stand in as the "On Call" doctor for all of my patients while I am away.

We take great family vacations. A well-known local DJ came in as a patient one day. He told me never to put off having great family vacations until later for any reason. He said kids grow up way too fast and before you know it, your opportunity to enjoy them is gone. I've done my best to follow his advice. Sometimes our vacations are just quick inexpensive four-day getaways and other times it's a plane trip to Disneyland. We plan to do humanitarian service trips to third world countries as the kids grow older and are more capable of understanding that they can make a positive difference in this world.

About three years ago, a millionaire real estate developer came to see me as a patient. He was eighty years young and oozed wisdom. I loved what he said about business. I almost felt guilty for having him pay for the dental work because I got so much value from what I learned listening to him speak. I'll never forget one day in particular. I had finished up a dental procedure and asked him to meet me in my office so we could chat a little before he left. After I took care of my last patient, I walked into my office and noticed him just standing there, staring at my family picture on the wall. He had a nostalgic look on his face as he stood there. I heard him mutter softly something like, "What I would give..." He explained how he and his wife had always thought they were too busy for having and raising kids. Too many projects to do, money to make and lists to check off. They'd put business and career ahead of family, and he had deep regrets for what might have been.

That day with my senior friend heavily reinforced that family comes first. My family comes first. Work, together with any business-related activities, is to be structured around our family lifestyle. Does everything always work that way? Of course not. However, this is the ideal I have chosen to strive for every day of my life. As a result, the monetary and non-monetary rewards have come in abundance...more than I could have imagined.

FAMILY CAMP-OUTS

One late summer day about five years ago, Jannie and I promised our two children we could have a camp-out in the back yard. We set up the tent and prepared for the big night. However, we left late in the day to visit some friends in a neighboring city. By the time we returned home, much to our children's disappointment, it was too dark, too late, and too cold outside. We told them we would make it up to them the next weekend and have our camp-out then.

The next Friday came and again it was too cold. Fall was in full swing and we realized we weren't going to have an ideal night for a camp-out in the back yard. So, we told the kids we'd have the camp-out in the family room instead. We pulled out the hide-a-bed, popped some popcorn, prepared their sippy cups and put on a movie to watch together. We let them stay up past their usual bedtime to enjoy the fun. We had a blast together. Little did Jannie and I know we'd started a family tradition that would continue each Friday night over the next 300 weeks and counting!

We still have a family camp-out every week. When Friday night hits, we pull out that hide-a-bed, get out the goodies, watch movies and stay up later than normal. Our six kids are in heaven and we are, too. In those moments, there's nowhere I'd rather be. I can't tell you how many times our little ones have asked, "Daddy? How many more days until Friday?" Now that the kids are getting older, even sleepovers at friends' houses are no competition for our family camp-outs. Creating family memories and enjoying those who mean the most to me is indeed helping me live my dream.

DAY WITH DAD

On Fridays at 3:30 p.m., my business world stops. I am home and ready to take one of my kids on a special outing with me. I cherished such outings with my own dad when I was a kid. Now it's my turn to pass it on to my children. I take each child in turn. We head off to do something special together for two or three hours. Sometimes we spend money and sometimes we don't. The important thing is that we spend quality one-on-one time together. It's my turn to make each child feel like the most important kid in the world. I love doing that and look forward to these moments we will cherish forever.

These special days have been such a positive experience for my children and me that we've decided to alternate and have special days with Mom, too. If it comes to spending "too much" time or giving "too much" attention to family, I prefer to err on the side of too much rather than not enough. It's an investment that consistently pays great dividends.

A Word About Chasing the Mighty Buck

I want to leave you with a thought one of my mentors left with me. Todd Vogel is the author of one of my favorite books, written exclusively for entrepreneur dentists. He is a true entrepreneur and teaches great principles of business success. He was very successful professionally and was compensated very well for it. But he learned a powerful lesson about seeking financial success. It's very simple:

A lot of money with no time is no better than a lot of time with no money.

The point here is never to lose the balance in the most important aspects of your life. Take time to smell the roses, enjoy the sunlight and relax in your own preferred way. I hope you are wildly successful as you seek to accomplish your goals. But whatever you do, never let a problem to be solved or money to be made take priority over someone to be loved.

A Final Note: Having It All

"The best way to predict the future is to create it."
— Peter Drucker

What are your odds of having it all? I hope you see now, more than ever before, your odds are greater than you ever imagined! You've read my story. What's your story? Maybe your story is just beginning. I hope this book has inspired you to dream big and make your life bigger than you ever thought possible. Because no matter whom you are or where you live, you were born to succeed and live a happy and successful life.

I hope you'll follow the success principles I outlined for you in this book. As I've said all along, these principles have been around for a long time because they work! I wish I could take credit for all of them, but they're not mine. I'm just an ordinary guy who wants to get the most out of life. I've decided to focus on success and abundance. You have the same ability, perhaps even more ability than I have.

When we're blessed with the opportunity to open our eyes on another day, we can choose the attitude we'll embrace that day. Will you choose an attitude that empowers you to make your dreams a reality? I believe you will!

Just the fact that you've read this book to the very end tells me you're ready and enthusiastic about beating all odds. Congratulations! Today is one you shouldn't forget. I promise, as you move forward and implement these strategies and ideas, your life will never be the same. Be sure to take a moment and celebrate this day. You deserve it and it's certainly good to be excited about the great things coming your way.

Now is the time. It's your time to shine. Quit getting ready to get ready. Get out there now and start on your dream life. Ready or not, get moving. You'll find tremendous power once you start taking action. After all, what you want in life wants you!

Will the journey be easy? At times it will, but then other times, it will be difficult. Remember, when the clouds of difficulty fog your vision and block out any hope of success, you are in control. Journey to higher ground! Read and re-read this book if you need some motivation during those tough times. Follow the principles of success every time and you will rise above the clouds of bitter cold into the warm bright sunshine of happiness and success.

The cover of this book represents the experience I shared during the introduction. If you don't remember, go back and re-read about that bitter cold Boise inversion day and what I did to get out of it. Within an hour of driving to higher ground, I came out of the clouds of fog into the warm sunshine and saw the thick white blanket of fog covering the entire valley below. As I stood at the top of the mountain that day, it all came together. Suddenly the entire message of this book became crystal clear. As you continuously journey to higher ground, you will be ever-empowered to rise above those clouds of discouragement and beat all the odds you might face in life.

Now that I've shared my philosophy with you, I encourage you to contact me to share your life dreams and successes. Please visit my web site at www.beatingallodds.com to contact me and take advantage of the resources I've made available for you there. I've already shared many of the lessons of this book with thousands of people. Little else makes me feel more fulfilled than to get a letter, an e-mail or a phone call telling me how what I said made somebody else's life better.

As you move forward in the journey to beat all odds, I'm going to leave you with a final challenge. Your success and happiness is not complete without the success and happiness of others. I hope you will go out of your way to ease the burdens and lighten the loads of many others. So your challenge is to make someone's day better today—this day. Remember, there's magic in it. You'll feel better, too.

This journey of beating any odds will not always be easy, but oh, it's worth every treacherous step. May you find success, happiness and fulfillment as you walk the journey of your life. May you become all you dream of becoming. May the lives of all you encounter be the better because of it. Thank you for allowing me to have a small role in your success!

Your friend,

Taylor Clark

WOULD YOU LIKE MORE?

Please visit my web site at www.BeatingAllOdds.com to take advantage of the free resources I've made available for you there. Feel free to return regularly for new resources as I discover them to help you beat the odds in business and life.

You can directly communicate with Dr. Clark online through his site.
He is also very active through online media:
Facebook: Taylor Clark

For information about having Dr. Clark speak to your
organization or group, please e-mail us at
DrClark@BeatingAllOdds.com

SHARE THE WEALTH

This book outlines the keys for people to thrive in any economy. My hope in writing this book is to empower you and thousands, perhaps even millions of people to become better than you ever thought possible. As each person raises his or her ability to succeed, the whole world benefits. We are all interdependent—a rising tide raises all boats—so why not share these success secrets with the rest of the world?

I therefore ask you to share this book of empowerment and hope with everyone you know. I invite you to tell at least twenty of your closest family members and friends about it or consider giving them this life-changing gift. I envision this world becoming a better place, one book, one person, one family at a time. Please help me make this dream become a reality.

ABOUT THE AUTHOR

Dr. Taylor Clark is an author, speaker, dentist, small business consultant and business entrepreneur whose passion is making life better for people. He has spent more than 16 years, intensely studying the field of personal growth and business development.

His business accomplishments have been recognized in newspapers, radio and television in many cities throughout the United States. He was recently named the 2009 Young Entrepreneur of the Year by the Boise Metro Chamber of Commerce.

Taylor founded *All About You Dental* in 2002, a multi-doctor dental practice that excels in cosmetic and family dentistry in Boise, Idaho.

In 2006, Dr. Clark founded the *Assist To Succeed* dental assisting school in Boise, Idaho. This lower cost accelerated Saturday course provides an excellent way for people to successfully enter the profession of dentistry without having to quit their jobs while in training. Shortly after starting this Boise-based school, Taylor decided to expand the program into other dental offices nationwide. Currently, over twenty-four dental offices throughout the U.S. have started the Assist To Succeed program.

He served a two-year volunteer church service mission in Southern Mexico and is fluent in Spanish. He has a strong financial background through his work in the securities industry. In 1998, he received his Bachelor of Science Degree from Brigham Young University with a minor in psychology. He received his Doctorate of Dental Surgery Degree from Creighton University in 2002. He has completed extensive continuing education since the conclusion of his formal schooling. He and his wife, Jannie, live in the Boise, Idaho area with their six children. Dr. Clark is 36 years old.

RECOMMENDED RESOURCES

SMILE BRIGHTER WILLOUGHBY HILLS

Smile Brighter Willoughby Hills is dedicated to the care and comfort of every person who crosses their threshold. The doctors and staff are committed to preventing and solving any dental problem you, your family, or your friends may have. We are also committed to spending valuable time with all of our patients—something increasingly rare in health care today. You will be dealing with members of a team whose primary job is to serve you. We love helping people feel better about themselves. In changing the lives of those we serve, we change our own.

Our purpose is to make life better for people. We help people maintain a high level of oral health and have beautiful smiles they can be proud of. Sharing valuable information and helping people make informed decisions helps us accomplish that goal. We have the interest and desire to listen – really listen – to what you are saying. Treating people how we ourselves would like to be treated ensures that our patients receive our very best care and attention. Everything we do is dedicated to the well-being and best interest of each person we serve.

We welcome you to visit our office for a free, no cost, no obligation, Five Star Healthy Smile Evaluation!
Call 440.975.8444 today and simply mention the
Beating All Odds special dental gift.

WWW.SMILEBRIGHTER.INFO

DENTAL ASSISTANT TRAINING PROGRAM

Assist To Succeed is a unique non-traditional way to become a dental assistant. It allows people to enter the profession of dentistry without going far into debt. This accelerated, lower cost dental assisting training course is held on Saturdays so people don't have to quit their current job for training. Students obtain a solid foundation in dental assisting with a strong hands-on emphasis. Course length and requirements vary from state to state. Typical course length is ten to twelve weeks.

Assist To Succeed was designed to go beyond simply teaching students a trade. Students gain self confidence, an optimistic attitude and the ability to succeed in all areas of their lives. This element of the training is unique to the program. Program graduates nationwide are enjoying high levels of personal and professional success.

Please visit www.AssistToSucceed.com to learn what doctors, students, and their parents say about the program. Please also note the many offices nationwide that offer the Assist To Succeed Program in their offices.

www.ASSISTTOSUCCEED.COM

ABOUT DAILYSUCCESSSTREAM

DailySuccessStream (DSS) is an online education company that offers cutting edge personal growth and business development for people in more than 100 countries worldwide. It offers an internet personal development library for entrepreneurs, salespeople, small-business owners, lifelong learners and anyone desiring to take their lives to the next level.

DSS leverages the street smarts and intellectual property of many of the most successful experts in the world in sales, marketing, management, entrepreneurship, tax and investment strategies, parenting, relationships, negotiating and many other areas. Content is delivered via the latest technology in the form of e-books, audio books and video to your PC, laptop or mobile device.

DSS offers content from many of the greatest teachers, authors, trainers, motivators and educators of our time including Brian Tracy, Bill Bartmann, Terri Murphy, Dan Clark, Dolf de Roos, Don Hutson, T. Harv Eker, Paula Fellingham, Jim Cathcart, John Gray, Hyrum Smith, Ivan Misner, Kevin Carroll, Debbie Allen, Mark Victor Hansen, Patricia Fripp, Marcia Petrie Sue, Sandy Botkin, Steve Siebold, Tom Ferry, Tony Alessandra, Chet Holmes, Trapper Woods, Leslie Householder, Paul Martinelli and more.

For more information about DailySuccessStream, and how you can use it to become better and more profitable in your current business or career, visit: www.BeatingAllOdds.com or go to: www.dailysuccessstream.com and sign up using the promo code: drclarkspecial to receive your first 5 days FREE. You may also go directly to the sign up page to receive the same offer at: http://members.dailysuccessstream.com/sign-up/drclarkspecial.

CUSTOMIZE THE RESOURCE PAGES FOR YOUR ORGANIZATION!

Use this book as a powerful contacting tool.

Share it with your prospects and become the mentor

they turn to when they're finished reading it!

Imagine YOUR contact information printed here!

Use the book as a lead generator for new sales team

members, distributors, clients, customers,

managers, leaders, etc.

Promote YOUR Company!

Visit www.BeatingAllOdds.com

to check on availability and terms

for the "Customize the Book" service.